financial
RESET

NANCY J. LAPOINTE, CFP®, MBA, ChFC®, CLU®, CASL®

financial
RESET

HOW YOUR *mindset*

ABOUT *money* AFFECTS YOUR

FINANCIAL *well-being*

Advantage®

Published by Advantage, Charleston, South Carolina.
Member of Advantage Media Group.

ADVANTAGE is a registered trademark and the Advantage colophon is a trademark of Advantage Media Group, Inc.

Printed in the United States of America.

ISBN: 978-1-59932-631-3
LCCN: 2015947208

Book design by Megan Elger.

This publication is designed to provide accurate and authoritative information in regard to the subject matter covered. It is sold with the understanding that the publisher is not engaged in rendering legal, accounting, or other professional services. If legal advice or other expert assistance is required, the services of a competent professional person should be sought.

Advantage Media Group is proud to be a part of the Tree Neutral® program. Tree Neutral offsets the number of trees consumed in the production and printing of this book by taking proactive steps such as planting trees in direct proportion to the number of trees used to print books. To learn more about Tree Neutral, please visit **www.treeneutral.com**. To learn more about Advantage's commitment to being a responsible steward of the environment, please visit **www.advantagefamily.com/green**

Advantage Media Group is a publisher of business, self-improvement, and professional development books and online learning. We help entrepreneurs, business leaders, and professionals share their Stories, Passion, and Knowledge to help others Learn & Grow. Do you have a manuscript or book idea that you would like us to consider for publishing? Please visit **advantagefamily.com** or call **1.866.775.1696**.

This book is for my people, clients, family, and friends.
In the words of Spock, "Live long and prosper."

PREFACE

Writing a book about money management and financial planning has been a goal of mine for many years. It has been fueled by my clients, their questions, and their deep concerns for themselves and those they love and care for.

In both my professional and private lives I have known countless people whose backgrounds and life experiences have not supported them in managing their finances effectively. Too many are actually living in fear of money, and in doing so, they are giving it a certain power over their lives. True, money is a reality in our world, but it should not control us.

My hope with this book is to help people see that they do not have to live in fear or avoidance. By understanding the concepts and following the practical suggestions I've provided, they can change their attitudes around money and come to feel a sense of empowerment and security when it comes to their finances.

Like almost every other book ever written—especially those written by people other than writers—this book has been possible thanks to the input, support, and technical assistance of several people. First, of course, is my mother, Carolyn Boggs, whose ongoing encouragement and belief in me are the foundation of my world. Without her practice of tough love balanced with her invaluable lessons of resilience and perseverance, I would never have undertaken—or completed—this project!

My life partner, Catherine LaPointe, has been 100 percent behind me in my career, my devotion to growth, and my willingness to take on challenges and risk. She has dealt with my myopic focus, long hours, and time spent on development with grace, patience, and humor.

Tammy J. Bond, friend and author, has exposed me to the do'ers and has inspired me to be more, do more, go outside my comfort zone, and take to the public arena. Her development as an international author and speaker was the catalyst for me to stop talking about it and start acting on my idea.

Without Tammy Chase's skills, faith, and commitment to our firm, Navigate Financial, this book could not possibly have happened. As my assistant and central office support person, she gave me the confidence and freedom to devote time to this project while knowing our clients would be cared for and the business would be in good hands.

I'd also like to acknowledge four people, each of whom has made a difference in my life: Denise Kerwin, whose friendship and family exposed me to a different way of living and being in this world and inspired ambition within me; Rick Cederberg, who was my mentor as I started this career and whose teachings still impact me today; Zale Crawford, my peer and motivator, who has encouraged me to keep improving and developing my skills now and over the years; and Jessica Jensen, with whom I have shared mutual support as we have grown our practices—hers in law, mine in financial planning—to be holistic and client-centered.

The Financial Planning Association (FPA)—the professional organization of which I am a member—and its powerful conference and networking opportunities, plus the vast energy and knowledge shared at its annual Million Dollar Round Table meeting, has had and continues to have a tremendous effect on my career and growth as a planner.

Susan Alexander, a skilled wordsmith and editor, has been fundamental in getting my ideas organized and the text ready for publication. Betsy Kelley is a creative graphic artist whose work and enthusiasm have been much appreciated.

Finally, I wish to recognize the team at Advantage Media Group, who got this book to print and helped make my long-held dream a reality.

Heartfelt thanks to you all!

FOREWORD

When did you first become aware of money? Can you remember your earliest financial references? Was it during the depression era of the '30s, the growth and optimism of the '50s, the glamour and excess of the '80s?

My first awareness of money was as a teenager (in the recession years of the '70s), when it was my dream to one day be able to buy whatever I wanted at the corner store without having to first count my money. And it has been that resolve—*to be able to spend without stress*—which has pretty much directed my financial choices throughout my life.

I believe most of us aspire to achieve that level of financial independence, and in *Financial Reset*, recognized financial planner Nancy LaPointe has provided the tools you need in order to accomplish this very goal.

To start charting a course for your own financial independence, it is helpful to first understand the genealogy and architecture of your current influences and tendencies. Of course, we all have very different money instincts and levels of financial flexibility and security, and no one tool or solution will suit every situation or personality. But Nancy LaPointe's book comes close.

A NEW SCIENCE

There is a relatively new field of study called *Neuroeconomics*, and in helping us understand our own spending habits, it can be very insightful. It is the interdisciplinary science that seeks to explain human decision making—the ability to process multiple alternatives, make the best selection, and follow a course of action. These decision-making skills are critical if we are to ultimately achieve financial independence and a sense of security.

Only within the last fifteen years have academics begun to look at how the interrelationship between sociology, behavioral science, and physiology influences our financial decision making. The good news is that the understanding of how our brain works—how it is impacted by the stresses and emotions of financial decisions—has enormous potential to help guide us through sound decision making. Sadly, however, this kind of knowledge also can be—and frequently is—used to manipulate consumers into excessive spending.

Perhaps you remember the scandals surrounding subliminal Coke images and single frame, popcorn ad inserts in the 1950s, which made us question who actually was in control of our spending. Now, fast-forward to today's gaming industry. Consider how it has been shaped by this new science as it has sought to develop effective ways of engaging players who are lured by hopes of a big payout. This is occurring every day.

The full potential of this new science is yet to be seen. But one thing we know is that just an *awareness* of the various factors that influence our decisions can keep us each in a better position to more effectively personalize our opportunities, anticipate our challenges, and stay on course while defending ourselves from unscrupulous predators.

What all this means is that you can benefit greatly by following a proactive and systematic approach toward managing your finances. *Financial Reset* goes a long way in helping you develop good habits of financial stewardship for yourself and your family.

BE GREEDY, BE FEARFUL

Albert Einstein said, "There are three great forces in the world: stupidity, fear, and greed. Stupidity (at least in hindsight) leads people into situations where fear and greed are the roots of their downfall." At some time or another, this might apply to all of us.

Decades later, Warren Buffet, the iconic investor, said "Be fearful when people are greedy and greedy when they are fearful." When people are greedy, bubbles happen. When they are fearful, they sell at low prices. Recognizing this can lead to wiser long-term investment strategies and tactics.

Watch your own emotions around *fear* and *greed* and observe how they may interact. Of the two, although it may seem coun-terintuitive, greed has been proven to be far and away the stronger of the two impulses. On one hand, greed is important to our economic system and drives us to do better. But it also can cause real damage, becoming unbridled and obscuring. After all, it is the basis of the lottery system, one of the most brilliant deceptions ever institutionalized.

So where is the right balance of greed and fear? Your personal history and financial "personality" combine to provide a comfort-able, natural set point for you, but that might not be the optimal mix you need to make the best financial decisions. Be aware of this dynamic, and manage your impulses so that they fall within your overall framework or plan.

Does this mean we should not trust our instincts? Well, yes … sort of. That's kind of the point, at least not until your instincts are properly honed and reflect both who you are today and the economic realities of the present world.

In *Financial Reset*, Nancy LaPointe gives you a workable, systematic approach to personal financial management. Using the organizational structure this book provides, you will be better prepared to fend off the extremes that *greed* and *fear* can exert on your financial life.

You have in your hands a valuable road map that can help you achieve financial independence. It is written in a way the reader can easily follow and deals intelligently with the many practical issues through which we all must navigate to succeed financially. Once you're set, pass this book along to others who can really use a great guide for their finances. Now, good luck on your journey!

CHARLES HAMOWY, CPA, CFP®
Coauthor of *Financially Secure Forever,*
The Seasons of Advice Solution

TABLE OF CONTENTS

INTRODUCTION

The longer I live, the more I realize the impact of attitude on life... I am convinced that life is 10 percent what happens to me and 90 percent how I react to it. And so it is with you... We are in charge of our attitudes.

—Charles Swindoll, American author, educator

If you're holding this book and reading these words, you probably have questions about money. Welcome to the masses of people who, like you, know they have questions—but don't have a good reliable source for answers.

I have answers about money. I ought to; I hold a master in business administration degree (MBA) and am a CERTIFIED FINANCIAL PLANNER™ practitioner (CFP®), a Chartered Financial Consultant (ChFC®), a Chartered Life Underwriter (CLU®), and a Chartered Advisor in Senior Living (CASL®). Within the coming year, I will be completing my Retirement Income Certified Professional (RICP®) as well. I have worked for 16 years with private clients, focusing on their money and financial security. Today in my financial planning practice, I help businesses, families, and individuals of all ages, from all walks of life—and with all levels of income—learn and incorporate sound money practices into their financial decision making.

You are the reason I acquired all this knowledge. You are smart and accomplished in your own field—as I am in mine—but your field is probably not financial planning, and that's why you have questions and why you're holding this book. (I'm sure I have questions about your field, if it makes you feel any better.) You want a basic understanding of financial planning, and you have the desire to learn, but you need a reliable, digestible, straightforward source of accurate information to help you make sound financial decisions that will support you in achieving the success you've envisioned.

In addition to answering your money questions, my other purpose in writing this book is to be a catalyst for change—in this case, a major, widespread attitude adjustment about money and how we use it. I realize this goal may be an ambitious one, but I believe strongly that too many people today experience financial problems because of unhealthy attitudes regarding money. They may know intellectually what they need and what their goals are, but when they make uneducated, risky choices based on the advice of friends or look for an immediate fix to their problems or leave decision making up to chance, it seriously compromises their financial security. In early 2015, Massachusetts Mutual Life Insurance Company (MassMutual) published the results of a study that found that "65 percent of Americans leave their financial well-being up to chance." Even in my own practice, I see people spending more time planning their vacations than their retirement.

You see, the cornerstone to my view of life is the concept that the only element in life over which we have full control is our attitude. I believe that our choices, our actions, and our outcomes are the result of how we view the world around us. I have seen over and over again how peoples' life choices are a reflection of their general attitudes and, in particular, of their attitudes toward money: spending money, saving money, earning money, paying money. I also believe that the change of attitude from fear, avoidance, and uncertainty to confidence, intentionality, and groundedness and to making decisions from a point of strength and self-assurance will be as life-changing to you as it has been for many of my clients.

In the following pages, I will describe various concepts on the topic of money, designed to help you understand it, develop an *intentional attitude* about it, and establish positive change in your financial decision making. Experience has shown me that change can only occur—and be effective and sustainable—if a person's attitude resonates with the directions or action steps being presented. In other words, without the mental and emotional framework of a defined money mind-set, even the most well-developed plan of action will simply be bound

When it's all said and done, you, and you alone, control your attitude.

**—Jeff Keller, author,
Attitude Is Everything**

pages of words and diagrams, lacking focus, cohesiveness, and purpose. I believe that if you read this book, refer to it as needed, and develop a positive and proactive money mind-set, you will be primed for the next step: building your financial house with a strong and sustainable structure to help you achieve success.

Our first step, in chapter 1, will be to familiarize you with your own money mind-set. You'll have the opportunity to reflect on some personal questions regarding how you perceive, spend, budget, and save money, and I'll offer guidance as you begin to identify your core goals, values, and priorities. We'll follow that in chapter 2 with basic, easy-to-understand definitions of money terms and concepts, such as cash flow, fixed costs, discretionary spending, price vs. value, and much more.

Chapter 3 will revert to asking questions, but these will be less about your habits and values and more about your current financial picture. I'll show you how to take a current "snapshot" of your assets, liabilities, and emergency preparedness—and how to assess how your recordkeeping may be impacting your finances.

Chapter 4 is one that I am particularly passionate about, and that is how to go forward from here with a healthy and intentional attitude about money—specifically, *your* money. We'll talk about breaking bad habits, clarifying short- and long-term goals, avoiding debt, and knowing when and how to say no to spending that does not support your intentions.

In chapter 5, you'll learn how to develop a budget, see how to reduce fixed expenses and debt, find numerous steps for saving money, and—perhaps most critically—align your personal core values with your spending patterns.

Chapter 6 is my gift to you: a plethora of money-saving tips and strategies from a veteran financial planner.

Finally, in chapter 7, we'll look at the future and consider some of the twists, turns, and opportunities that may lie ahead. We'll explore some of the positive and negative aspects of retirement, and we'll discuss ways to educate your children in order to reinforce positive money attitudes as they start out in their own lives.

I encourage you to take it slowly as you're progressing from one section to the next, from one topic to the next. Take small bites. Chew on them for a while before moving on. Go back frequently and reread sections, as it will help in grasping new material. I also encourage you to consider your own personality, work habits, and relationship dynamics as you develop specific tactics to implement the strategies presented. Throughout the book, I'll make suggestions and share approaches that others have used to meet their objectives, as there is no single, universal way for everyone to apply these concepts.

I venture to say that many readers have made financial decisions without going about them using an intentional and mindful process. They may not reflect your core values or reinforce one another to achieve optimal results. You may be confused, intimidated, or frustrated, or perhaps you're looking for a magic bullet to address your financial concerns. The bottom line is that it takes time to develop a new plan and head in a new direction. The journey you're on is always subject to change; it's an organic process with frequent curveballs and an occasional need for adjustments. Keeping that in mind, use this book and the suggestions I offer to design strategies to shape your own financial attitude and strengthen your chances for stability, security, and peace of mind.

CHAPTER 1

Getting to Know your Money Mindset

If a person gets his attitude toward money straight, it will help straighten out almost every other area in his life.

—Billy Graham, American evangelist and spiritual advisor

IT'S ALL ABOUT ATTITUDE

I have a favorite little motivational quote that invariably gets posted on Facebook every few months. Beside a cartoon drawing of a discouraged young boy wearing a baseball cap is a bicycle that has no air in one of its tires. The bicycle is lying on the ground, useless. Beneath the drawing are the words "A bad attitude is like a flat tire. Until you change it, you can never go anywhere."

Most of us, myself included, have learned that our day-to-day attitudes toward people, things, events—or just life in general— can help or hinder us in countless ways. Negative, downbeat attitudes can limit us, annoy our spouses, turn off our friends, and possibly get us fired. As we'll get into later, they also can lead to misguided beliefs and thought processes when it comes to our finances. Positive, *can do* attitudes, on the other hand, are better for our health, appealing to others, contagious, and they can change the world in fantastic ways! Starting with your own, which is *the only one you can control*, you can change *your* world.

Where do our attitudes come from? They often are rooted in how we've been raised, what we've experienced, what we value, and how we feel about ourselves. In other words, to borrow a popular phrase from the '70s, our attitudes are a reflection of "where we're coming from."

In the same way our core values and the sum of our experiences will dominate our general attitude toward life, people, places, problems, and so on, they also will shape our financial attitudes. If you're working with a negative or avoidance money mind-set, or if you've adopted beliefs and behaviors based on avoidance and negativity, you aren't using the best tools available. And you are working without specific intention. What that means, in a financial context, is that your actions will likely be defaults and reactions, and your decision making may be haphazard, inconsistent, and emotionally driven. There is no constructive philosophical framework driving your decision making. But a positive, self-defined money mind-set—or *financial attitude*—can be key to meaningful, proactive, financial choices that will support your short- and long-term goals.

> *Attitude is defined as a way of looking at or viewing life. This is why attitude has been described as the "control center" of your life. Your attitude is a decision, and it is a learned behavior.*
>
> **—Jim Afremow, PhD, LPC, author of *Trust the Talent***

Despite your values and attitudes developing from an early age and in a deep place within you, they do not necessarily have to remain the same throughout your life. *You can evolve.* You can change your perspectives, adjust your attitude, and, in turn, have more control over your behaviors, choices, and outcomes. In fact, as mentioned a moment ago, the one thing you have control over in your life *is your attitude.*

Becoming more enlightened, and learning more about the world, can help to broaden and improve your basic attitude. And so it is with money. Understanding it, and knowing how to manage it, will help you to develop a positive, healthy money mind-set. "Your mind is a computer that can be programmed," writes coach and trainer Keith Harrell in "Why Your Attitude Is Everything and How to Turn It Into Action," an article in the May 2009 issue of *Success Magazine.* "You can choose whether the software installed is productive or unproductive. Your inner dialogue is the software that programs your attitude, which determines how you present yourself to the world around you. You have control over the programming. Whatever you put into it is reflected in what comes out."

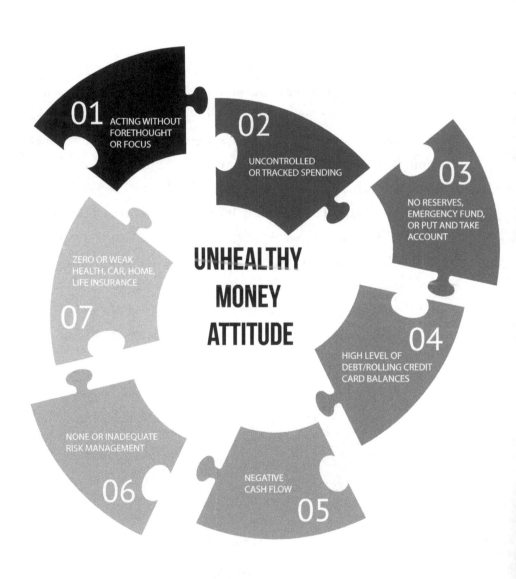

01 ACTING WITHOUT FORETHOUGHT OR FOCUS

02 UNCONTROLLED OR TRACKED SPENDING

03 NO RESERVES, EMERGENCY FUND, OR PUT AND TAKE ACCOUNT

UNHEALTHY MONEY ATTITUDE

04 HIGH LEVEL OF DEBT/ROLLING CREDIT CARD BALANCES

05 NEGATIVE CASH FLOW

06 NONE OR INADEQUATE RISK MANAGEMENT

07 ZERO OR WEAK HEALTH, CAR, HOME, LIFE INSURANCE

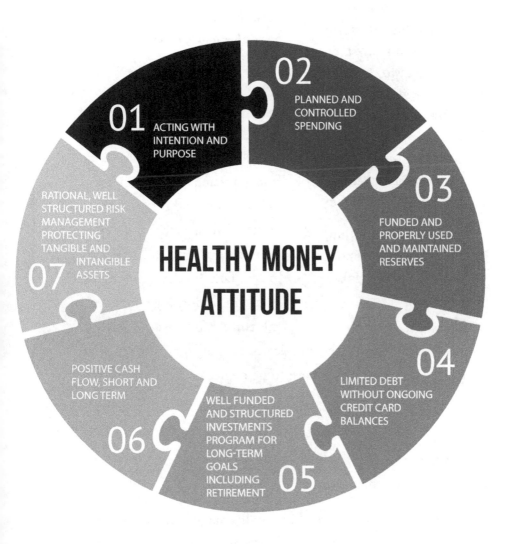

01 ACTING WITH INTENTION AND PURPOSE

02 PLANNED AND CONTROLLED SPENDING

03 FUNDED AND PROPERLY USED AND MAINTAINED RESERVES

04 LIMITED DEBT WITHOUT ONGOING CREDIT CARD BALANCES

05 WELL FUNDED AND STRUCTURED INVESTMENTS PROGRAM FOR LONG-TERM GOALS INCLUDING RETIREMENT

06 POSITIVE CASH FLOW, SHORT AND LONG TERM

07 RATIONAL, WELL STRUCTURED RISK MANAGEMENT PROTECTING TANGIBLE AND INTANGIBLE ASSETS

HEALTHY MONEY ATTITUDE

> *The only way to permanently change the temperature in the room is to reset the thermostat. In the same way, the only way to change your level of financial success "permanently" is to reset your financial thermostat. But it is your choice whether you choose to change.*
>
> **—T. Harv Eker, author, businessman, and motivational speaker**

IT STARTS WITH SELF

The difference between a successful person and others is not a lack of strength, not a lack of knowledge, but rather a lack of will.

—Vince Lombardi (1913–1970)
Head coach of the Green
Bay Packers, 1959–1967

We're all different. We come from different places, different upbringings, and different viewpoints. We may exert different influences or serve different roles in our families or communities. But as the old saying reminds us, the three things we do have in common are money, taxes, and death. Like attitude, the only one of the three over which we have some degree of control is money.

An Allianz Life Insurance Company survey done in November 2014 revealed that for most of the people surveyed, getting in shape was a bigger priority than improving their finances.[1]

To be truly healthy—physically, intellectually, emotionally, and spiritually—is to exist in a place of strength and to be free of any

---

1   "6th Annual Allianz Life New Year's Resolution Survey," allianz.com. December 08, 2014.

debilitating, progressive diseases. **To be financially healthy is no different. Like your body, if you neglect, mismanage, or mistreat your money, you'll face negative consequences down the road.** But there needs to be a close alignment between the two. If you are physically and intellectually strong yet financially weak, you are not positioned to live your best life. If you are financially strong but physically and emotionally hurting, the quality of your life is also compromised. If we each paid a fraction of the attention to our financial health as we do to our physical fitness, our lawns, and our vehicles and other assorted toys, I believe we all would be on the road to an improved, healthier life. It takes desire, a conscious effort, and yes, time.

Too often in our busy lives, we neglect things we shouldn't. Starting today, why not commit yourself to addressing and integrating all areas of your life and to finding the tools, activities, and support systems that will allow you to become the healthiest you can be? Spend quality time with your family members and friends. Be there for them in ways that are meaningful to them. Try to limit the junk food and channel surfing, and instead, develop—and stick to—good eating habits, a sustainable exercise program, and a regular routine of satisfying activities. Find stimulating people to be with and other ways that can help you stay intellectually sharp. And in your financial life, understand where your money is coming from, take care of what you have, and work at building stability for yourself and your family. Only about 10 percent of boomers are "highly engaged in their financial lives," says Ron Shevlin, author of the 2012 Aite Group report on money management. Are you? This is your one life. Be and do your best. Live not by default but with intention.

> *What to do isn't the problem; doing it is. Most of us know what to do, but we just don't do it. If I can control the guy in the mirror, I can be skinny and rich.*
>
> **—Dave Ramsey, author of *The Total Money Makeover Classic Edition: A Proven Plan for Financial Fitness* (2013)**

WHAT DOES MONEY DO FOR YOU?

> *I think at the end of the day you have to find a balance with what's really important.*
>
> —Julianne Hough, musician and dancer

Do you ever think about the overall purpose of the money you work hard for? It may be difficult to come up with a streamlined and straightforward answer, as money covers a multitude of varying—and, at times, mutually exclusive—wants and needs. But you must know what is more important to you: Is it to enhance your lifestyle, or is it to simply survive? It is never easy making consistently sound decisions when it comes to spending, saving, or investing money. Not understanding our purpose makes it near impossible. We owe it to ourselves to reflect regularly on those priorities and to have a basic sense of what comes before everything else.

Let's say I have two neighbors, Pete and Paul. Both have shared with me over the years their desire to stop being renters and to purchase a home. This is a dream they have in common with many in our community.

Pete spends 45 percent of his monthly income on entertainment and travel and, therefore, has saved very little toward a down payment on a house. Sure, Pete's doing well and is having a great time, but he's no closer to reaching his goal of owning his own home than he was the day he was handed his college diploma. It might be ten or twenty years before he can accumulate what he will need to purchase a home.

Paul has always dreamed of buying a home before he turns thirty. Every month, he puts more than half of his paycheck into a savings account for his down payment. Unfortunately, with little to no extra spending money, when Paul wants a social life or needs a vacation, he uses credit cards to cover his expenses. He'll be a homeowner before long, but he'll have some hefty credit card debt to go along with his mortgage, and this consumer debt can influence the interest rate he is offered.

Both Pete and Paul would be wise to take some time to define their goals. It is possible that for Pete, travel and entertainment are actually more important and more fulfilling than owning a home of his own. Perhaps Paul ought to extend his home ownership deadline and avoid getting himself into high-interest debt. Working with a framework of defined objectives, both men are more likely to make spending choices that will reflect their values and bring satisfaction to their lives.

When I speak to groups, I often refer to money as **"the dispassionate enabler of whatever is meaningful to us."** It has no purpose or meaning in and of

Nearly 80% of more than 2,100 people admitted that their personal finances keep them awake at night.

—The National Foundation of Credit Counseling Financial Literacy Opinion Index posted on its website, debtadvice.org, throughout July 2014

itself. It can serve a purpose for you, or it can serve as a master. How you manage your relationship with money and organize your life around money will determine what your options are.

How do you determine your expenditures—on an as-you-go basis or as a response to ongoing opportunities or to fulfill the goals and visions you have for your life? Unless your answer is the latter, this may be a good time to re-evaluate. Make the decision to start living purposefully and begin proactively managing the tool that subsidizes your choices and enables you to live with options and flexibility. Position yourself to be able to achieve a sense of accomplishment and fulfillment by living a life reflective of your values.

When you live your life with definition and intention, you have a built-in set of guidelines that help you make better choices. You have a compass to determine whether an action or expenditure will support your goals. You can make decisions as part of a cohesive picture rather than in a vacuum with no strategic direction. If your number-one priority is to spend as much time with your kids as possible, then the financial choices you make should enable you to do that. Resist that higher-paying job in the next county, or you'll be spending more time in your car than with your kids. If your life's dream is to study culinary arts and become a chef, then think about whether that new, expanded cable package will do much to help you get there. If being involved in your kayaking group feeds your soul, why are you working extra hours to afford a luxury SUV?

WHAT DRIVES YOU?

Money is only a tool. It will take you wherever you wish, but it will not replace you as the driver.

—Ayn Rand

I know a woman who on a regular basis satisfies her personal wants by purchasing things she *wants* for her home, her family, and herself. I also know her husband, and he is more likely to spend money only when it's going to satisfy a definite, practical *need*—a new roof, for example, to protect his real estate investment or a washing machine when the old one has spun its last rinse cycle. I have often imagined these two having some "interesting discussions" over how they spend their money. Then again, they may be one of the 91 percent of couples who find reasons to avoid talking about finances, as reported in the *American Express Spending and Saving Tracker report* (2010).

What about you? Are you more like the wife or the husband in the scenario above? Are you driven by *needs* or *wants* when it comes to spending money? Needs, of course, are what we *have to have*—items and tools required for us to survive, as well as food, shelter, and clothing. Wants are our *desires*, enhancements, and entertainment. Put this way it seems easy to differentiate between the two, yet we struggle and act as if needs are wants and wants are needs. There truly is no right or wrong in what motivates us, in and of itself. While most of us lean more toward one side than the other and know which side that is, the actual process of deciding whether or not to make a purchase remains a complicated and daunting one. Almost all of us have some level of internal relationship struggles between our wants and our needs.

NEEDS VS. WANTS

Needs are essentials:

» Food

» Shelter

» Clothing

» Transportation

Wants are extras:

» Eating out

» Big, expensive house

» Shop till you drop

» Brand-new or expensive car

In their work on the psychology of choice, A. Tversky and D. Kahneman found that logic is not the driver when it comes to decision making. They reported that, instead, how the circumstances of the decisions are set up or framed has a more significant impact. We struggle not only within ourselves but also with our family members and business partners as we attempt to make choices and understand our motives. **Rationalization is a challenge when making purchasing decisions. We are very good at justifying our behavior, and this is often manifested by confusing needs with wants.**

Financial arguments most often are over differing opinions of "needs" versus "wants," with 58 percent of those who argue about money identifying this issue as the most common cause.[2]

When we are driven by our wants and struggle with that regularly, it helps to try seeing the larger picture. You *want* a new rug today because it would perk up the hallway and cover the damaged floor tiles. But resisting the *want*, and perhaps holding off a few more months, could allow you to replace the hallway

---

2 "AICPA Survey: Finances Causing Rifts for American Couples," May 4, 2012.

floor, which you know you *need* to repair. The rug, though beautiful, would delay the required repair by funneling resources to a temporary situation and masking the actual problem.

Some of us are more needs driven in our motivation. A young father is in graduate school for the certification he *needs* for his next promotion. He also *needs* to purchase supplies and equipment he will use on the job. Although it's going to cost him, these are things he *needs*. It sounds like he has his priorities straight. Yet, he must be careful to avoid the trap of repeatedly denying his personal wants until he loses both patience and perspective and ends up spending way more than he should have on something he *wanted* that in the long run wasn't all that important.

> *Some habits of ineffectiveness are rooted in our social conditioning toward quick-fix, short-term thinking.*
>
> —**Stephen Covey**, author, ***7 Habits of Effective People***

Something I encourage my clients to do when considering a major purchase is to make a list of what they need and want out of the purchase, whether it's a car, home, vacation, etc. Then I suggest they start their research process and refer back to the list they created. This practice helps temper "buyer drift," otherwise known as impulse buying or accessory purchases. Mackenzie Maher, author of *Wants vs. Needs: The Secret to Successfully Prioritizing Your Expenses* (2013), goes one step further. She recommends you create an overall list of your personal wants and needs, as an individual or a couple, and then use the list to reduce your brain playing tricks on you, and modifying a want into a need.

LET THERE BE TWO

Marriage, at the bottom, is an economic arrangement. It is a contract.

—H.L. Mencken, "The Sage of Baltimore," columnist

 Then there are those of us in marriages and domestic partnerships in which the partners reside together and share expenses but frequently don't agree on where the money should go. It is not an understatement to say the two partners' conflicting motivators can present a persistent challenge.

Forty percent believe their partner spends more money than they do on things outside of household expenditures. The same number (40 percent) consider themselves more diligent than their partner when it comes to saving money and budgeting.[3]

Larry and Liz are a classic example. The wants that fuel Larry, a lifelong model train enthusiast, seem alien and altogether unnecessary to Liz, who was raised in poverty in the slums of a large city. Liz believes that every purchase they make should fit somehow into the couple's long-range plans of early retirement. She maintains a written timeline and monitors it frequently, which generates a sense of comfort and promotes a feeling of well-being for her. Larry has little understanding of her need for strict record-keeping. He'd be a lot more comfortable with a flexible timeline and occasional splurges at the Model Railroad Hobby Shop, just for fun. His impatience with her austerity and her frustration with

---

3   American Express Spending and Saving Tracker survey, 2010

his lack of support sometimes create tension within their relationship—tension that finds its way into other aspects of their life together.

Three-quarters (76 percent) of those surveyed believe they share the same philosophy as their partner when it comes to managing money, such as saving versus spending. Younger couples are less likely to believe this is true, with only two-thirds (63 percent) of those between 25–34 and less than half (47 percent) of those between the ages of 18–24 feeling like thcy are on the same page as their partner financially.[4]

But fortunately, Larry and Liz recognize that their two different approaches are reflections of their personal style and not necessarily a deal-breaker. The fact is that different paths and motivational traits can actually be

What's the Problem?

Social psychologist Dr. Terri Orbuch of the University of Michigan has been conducting a longitudinal study, funded by the National Institutes of Health, since 1986, involving 373 same-race couples. She has reported that money is the number-one point of conflict in the majority of marriages she has studied, good or bad.

Underscoring that, University of Georgia academics McCoy, Ross, and Goetz reported in the *Journal of Financial Therapy,* Volume 4, Issue 2, 2013, that about one-third of the couples who are in marital therapy report financial stressor problems.

---

4   Capitol One survey, 2009

empowering for a couple. Their contrasting attitudes can be effective in maintaining a healthy balance when it comes to working and making spending decisions together. The key is to communicate and acknowledge the differences. In some instances, "taking turns" or "agreeing to disagree" is a healthy way of handling the problem. This time, resist the temptation to make a purchase, and next time perhaps you can treat yourselves. Just keep in mind that some behavior is hard-wired and some will be circumstantial,

> Dr. Hersh Shefrin at Santa Clara University's Leavey School of Business cites strong evidence that nature (i.e., genetics) impacts financial decision making, just as it does athletic ability and physical traits.

both for you and for your partner. Demonstrating both flexibility and understanding of the other will go far as you build a mutually supportive path and keep tensions at bay. Try using a scale of one to ten to express the strength of conviction to make a purchase or to do an activity. "10" is a burning desire and "1" is a whim. This method can reduce tension, while allowing everyone to be heard.

YOUR CORE VALUES: THE NITTY GRITTY

Try not to become a man of success but rather try to become a man of value.

—Albert Einstein (1879–1955), physicist and Nobel laureate

As individuals, whether we are always aware of them or not, most of us have a core set of values—the personal beliefs and ideals that guide our lives and decision making. Couples, too, can have core values, along with shared interests and goals. Reflection allows us to define and articulate values. While often adjusting to changes and varying circumstances, our values remain somewhat consistent, providing a barometer against which to measure, or evaluate, our actions and the choices we make. **Values reflect the "why." They give meaning to our activities and are the motivation to our goals.** Whatever our values are, our income goals and expenditures are typically centered around supporting them. The type of housing we live in, our food budgets, our entertainment and travel choices, and even the hours and type of employment we seek, should be aligned with our values. Too often, we are busy reacting to others and we stop listening to ourselves. Our actions become disconnected from our values. Without alignment, our values become empty token expressions—words without meaning. We become adrift without principles to guide us—subject to impulsive flights of fancy and impractical short-term decisions that will have long-term effects and consequences.

Values develop whether we are conscious of them or not, yet without introspection and recognition they may not be consistently acted upon, and our choices won't reflect them. Too often, people live their lives as a series of reactive behaviors, without acknowledging how their decisions are being made and what impact they may be having. By not defining our core personal values, we may be setting ourselves up for a chaotic financial life, filled with frustration, indecision, and regret. Living our lives in ways that are consistent with our values and expectations can lead to self-acceptance, consistency, and inner peace.

As an example, Noel is someone for whom education is a basic and essential part of life. He thrives when he is exposed to new ideas and concepts. He longs for the intellectual challenge and exciting potential of an executive-level position. Earning an advanced degree has long been at the top of his bucket list. Yet, with a full-time job, two growing children, a large house with an even larger lawn, and numerous community commitments, the likelihood that Noel will ever resume his education and earn his degree is small. The day may come when Noel realizes he has all but abandoned his dreams, but before it does, his very full life could instead feel very empty and unsatisfying.

I would advise Noel to begin a journey of introspection and self-examination in order to recognize his most basic beliefs and sort out what his true values are. Is his midlevel management job giving him a sense of accomplishment and fulfillment, or are his long work hours robbing him of the opportunity to seek a more satisfying position he could qualify for with an advanced degree? Are the relentless demands of his family, house, and yard denying him the chance to realize his potential and become what he dreams of becoming? In other words, is he living his life and making his choices in alignment with his values? To quote Walt Disney's older brother, Roy, who financed the cartoonist's earliest efforts, "It's not hard to make decisions when you know what your values are."

Life is short. Take the time you need to determine what your core values are. Then start taking steps to align your actions with your values.

KNOW THYSELF!

Until you make peace with who you are, you'll never be content with what you have.

—Doris Mortman, American author

Wouldn't it be wonderful if we each came with our own instruction book? It would explain in precise detail how we work as unique individuals: what we need, what we like, what we should avoid, and what motivates us. At the back of the book would be a complete maintenance program to keep us in good working order and ensure that we find joy and satisfaction in every activity of our lives.

Inconveniently, no such manual exists. It is up to each of us to do the work of self-reflection and self-evaluation that will provide the clues to achieving our best lives. Knowing ourselves is an ongoing and ever-changing process; as we move from one phase of our lives to the next, we must expect that we will grow, change, and evolve. Once we have a grasp of who we are and what our own truths and values are, then we can almost write our own instruction manuals.

Let me caution you, however. In an effort to understand ourselves, we often try to label and categorize ourselves. Am I a saver or a squanderer? A tightwad or a spend thrift? It's not that simple. We humans are much too complex to be divided into simple, clear-cut classifications. Besides, in researching the impact of nature vs. nurture, Dr. Hersh Shefrin, of Santa Clara University's School of Business, asserts that just 33 percent of spending habits are due to genes, so nurture wins the day.

We would serve ourselves better by examining our general tendencies and identifying predominant patterns of behavior. For example, ask yourself what you have done in your life that has brought you the most happiness. What choices and decisions have you made that worked out the best? At the same time, acknowledge which behaviors have *not* been constructive, which choices have *not* helped get you to your goals. Reaching back into your past can be helpful, while again keeping in mind that you have grown and evolved through the years. For many, professional counseling, support groups, and self-help books can facilitate the process. Bottom line: A program of self-awareness starts and ends with each individual, and it is one of the greatest gifts you can give yourself.

Because I believe you can only achieve your life goals if you take the time to explore your values and your patterns of behavior around money, the following are questions I invite you to read and ponder on your journey toward self-knowledge. Space is provided for those who would like to jot down thoughts and ideas. There are, of course, no right or wrong answers. Most important in this exercise is that you be truthful with yourself.

- Do you enjoy spending money? What kinds of purchases are pleasurable and which ones are painful?

A theory set forth in 2007 by academics Rick, Cryder, and Loewenstein proposed that savers spend less than what they would like to because of the pain they are dealing with, and savers are hard-wired to spend less. Spenders, they proposed, are not dealing with this pain at the same level and spend more. Extreme savers and spenders exist based on the levels of stimuli their INSULA area deals with.

—"Tightwads and Spendthrifts" (2007) Rick, Cryder, and Loewenstein, *Journal of Consumer Research*

- How do you feel when you've made a very large purchase? Proud? Excited? Guilty? Regretful?

- What purchases in your life have brought you the most joy? Why did they feel so good?

- What purchases have you regretted in the past? Why do you feel regret now?

- Does it take you a long time to buy something you need?

- Do you ever use coupons to save money or go to stores known for good deals and hefty markdowns? If yes, how do you feel when you have saved money?

- Do you have an older car with thousands of miles on it, or are you driving a newer model that's fully loaded? Is this consistent with your past vehicles? What are your reasons for driving the type of car you have?

- Do you enjoy taking vacations and consider them money well spent?

- What types of social activities do you most enjoy, and what types do you prefer to avoid?

- How important are cultural activities to you? How often do you attend plays, concerts, or the ballet? Do you attend as much as you would like to?

- Does the amount of money you spend on a trip or activity impact how much you enjoy yourself?

- When the going gets rough, do you go shopping? Is retail therapy helpful to you in dealing with the ups and downs of life?

- Finally, if you had it to do all over again, what expensive items would you purchase again and what would you live without?

CHAPTER 2

GETTING TO KNOW ABOUT MONEY

An investment in knowledge pays the best interest.

—Benjamin Franklin, American author, politician, statesman, scientist, inventor, and civic activist

Before trying to reshape your money attitude, it would be smart to stop and ask yourself how comfortable you are around the subject of money. To what extent do you understand the basic concepts, the vocabulary of money? Are you confident in your knowledge? Do you know clearly who is boss—you or your money? In a professional or social setting, do your eyes glaze over when the topic of conversation changes to compounded interest or economic fluctuation?

Money is like a sixth sense, without which you cannot make complete use of the other five.

—W. Somerset Maugham, British playwright, novelist, and short story writer

On the following pages is a sort of reference glossary, developed with you in mind. Don't be nervous; it's not advanced economic theory, and you won't be quizzed at the end. I think you'll find it accessible, digestible, and helpful, both today as you're reading it and in the future when you come back and refer to it. The terms below are purposely not listed in alphabetical order. Instead, they are arranged in a sequential order (i.e., once you understand one concept, you'll be ready to move to the next, and so on). An alphabetical index for easy referencing can be found at the end of the glossary.

It all starts with …

> What is MONEY? A piece of PAPER, a chunk of METAL, or just some bits and bytes.
>
> …
>
> It can give you the power to say YES and the freedom to say NO.
>
> It's EVERYTHING … and NOTHING.
>
> Because MONEY is just money.
>
> —Harmon Okinyo, African Poet

MONEY

Money is the exchange medium that is used to pay for time, skills, services, and/or products that we provide or purchase. It is a concept used by most modern societies in one form or another to compensate for efforts and goods given or received. People earn money in order to buy the services and products they need or desire in their lives. While for many centuries various coins and printed paper primarily served as money, today's technologies have allowed numerous other forms of "money" to be used more frequently (e.g., checks, credit cards, online payment systems, "bitcoin," and others).

INCOME

The money you receive when you work at your job, provide services, or sell goods or property is your income. You also may receive income in the form of profit from investments, such as rental income from a house you may own or income from a mutual fund you purchased. Income is frequently measured within a defined period of time (e.g., annual income, monthly income).

> *Many folks think they aren't good at earning money, when what they don't know is how to use it.*
>
> **—Frank A. Clark, American writer and cartoonist**

GROSS INCOME

The amount of your income before taxes, Social Security, and other deductions are taken out is your gross income. This is not the final dollar amount written on your paycheck that you are depositing in the bank.

NET INCOME

There are two contexts in which this term is used. First is the amount of money that you receive in the form of your paycheck—what you consider your take-home pay—after your taxes and other deductions are taken out. Second, it is used to refer to the dollar amount you have remaining, after you pay all your bills and satisfy all your financial commitments, to add to your savings and to use for non-necessities.

CASH FLOW

Cash flow is a term that describes how your money moves into and out of your life within a specific time period. It refers to the

amount of cash you have available after you have paid your bills and purchased what you need. Whether you have positive or negative cash flow is a reflection of how well you manage your finances and live within your means. Read more about cash flow on page 110 and see cash flow diagrams below.

> *The fact is that one of the earliest lessons I learned in business was that balance sheets and income statements are fiction, cash flow is reality.*
>
> **—Chris Chocola, American businessman**

Positive: More in than out. You are living with the ability to not just survive but thrive.
Negative: Struggling, will crash eventually, without financial strength or resilience.

BUDGET

A budget is a specific, customized plan that guides how an individual, family, business, or organization will spend their money within a specific time period. Budgets, which typically reflect monthly or annual spending, are usually itemized in distinct spending categories and are reconciled at the end of the time period to determine how closely the spending plan was followed. *See chapter 5 for samples of budgets.*

FIXED EXPENSES

1. Fixed

The ongoing expenses that are consistent and unlikely to change from one time period to the next are your fixed expenses. In a household budget, for example, fixed monthly expenses could include a rent or mortgage payment, child support payments, insurance premiums, property taxes, daycare tuition, student loan payments, and membership dues.

VARIABLE EXPENSES

2. Variable

Variable expenses are expenses that are not covered in one's regular fixed costs. They may include exceptions to one's regular fixed costs. Some examples of variable expenses are food, household expenses, remodeling projects, vacations, holiday costs, one-time charitable donations, gifts, and large purchases.

EXPECTED EXPENSES

If your car insurance is paid every six months rather than monthly, that is a *known or expected expense* that you can be setting money aside for (i.e., putting one-sixth of your total insurance premium into a savings account every month). New tires on your vehicle, roof replacement costs, house painting, and lawn maintenance are other examples of expected expenses you can anticipate and be prepared for in order to avoid a panic situation.

DISCRETIONARY SPENDING

3. Discretionary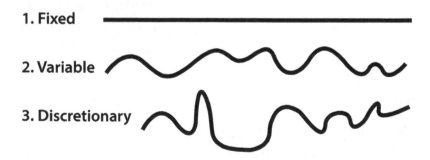

The term discretionary spending refers to purchases that are not essential for your well-being, safety, or security. They are usually items that you can live without but that enhance your life and contribute to your comfort, enrichment, and enjoyment. Costs related to clothing, entertainment, travel, recreation, and charitable gifts are good examples of discretionary spending.

According to the Experian *2011 Discretionary Spend Report,* the typical American household has $12,800 in annual discretionary spending.

1. Fixed ─────────────────

2. Variable

3. Discretionary

EMERGENCY FUND

An emergency fund is an amount of money you have set aside, probably in a savings account, to help you handle the unexpected and sometimes unpleasant twists and turns of life. Ideally, it is equivalent to three to six months of overall living expenses.

Illnesses, accidents, burglaries, and catastrophic acts of nature can come out of nowhere and have a detrimental impact on your financial stability and your ability to recover quickly. Having sufficient funds to get you through an extended illness, or taking money from an emergency fund to cover an insurance deductible, are good uses of emergency money.

 Only 38 percent of American adults have an emergency fund to fall back on.[5]

PRICE

Price is the dollar amount you are asked to pay if you want to purchase an item or service. It is the amount determined by the seller that he wants to receive for the products or services he is providing.

VALUE

A much more personal concept, value refers to how much the service or product is worth *to you* at the price it is marked. Does it enhance your life? Fill a need? Fix a problem? For example, if you need more seating in your living room and find a perfect chair that is marked $500, you may decide you are not willing to spend $500 because it isn't worth it to you at that price. But when the same chair is reduced to half-price, it now may have greater value—feel more worth it—to you.

---

5   "American Family Financial Statistics," April 27, 2015. www.statisticbrain.com/american-family-financial-statistics.

CREDIT

This is a term with several meanings. First, if you pay your bills and make your loan payments on time, you will build and maintain good *credit*—as scored and reported by consumer *credit bureaus*—and stores and businesses will be willing to loan you money in the future. Good *credit scores* often mean you can borrow money at lower interest rates. A *credit card* is used to make a purchase when you do not have

the cash available to pay for it; payments are then made monthly until the purchase is paid for. Finally, if you have a *store credit*, then it means the store owes you money. This happens when a store accepts a returned item but will only give you *credit* for it, as opposed to cash. *Creditors* are those who have extended credit to you and to whom you now owe money.

> *Every time you borrow money, you're robbing your future self.*
>
> —Nathan W. Morris, author, personal finance expert

DEBT

Debt refers to money you owe to others—to individuals, businesses, or banks. When you borrow money for college, purchase a car with a car loan, or buy a house with a mortgage, you incur debt. The more quickly you repay these loans, the sooner you will be out of debt. See also, **Interest.**

ASSETS

All that you have and own are your assets. Your savings, property, vehicles, jewelry, art, stocks, and mutual funds are all considered your assets. Tangible assets are divided into *appreciable* and *depreciable assets*. Homes usually *appreciate* (increase in value) over time; automobiles *depreciate* (decrease in value) over time. The portion of your home that is paid for is considered an asset. Your assets are considered *liquid assets* when you can easily exchange them for cash; land or homes are considered *illiquid assets* because they usually cannot be exchanged for cash in a short amount of time.

LIABILITIES

What you owe to others—your total **debt**—is considered your liability. The dollar amounts outstanding on short- and long-term loans, as well as what you owe to stores for items ordered or purchased, are your liabilities.

> *If you would be wealthy, think of saving as well as getting.*
>
> —Benjamin Franklin (1706–1790)

NET WORTH

Very simply, your assets minus your liabilities equal your net worth. It's what is left when you do not owe money to anyone. At times in your life, your net worth can be expected to be *negative* (e.g., when you have recently graduated from college and have a student loan to repay, so your liabilities are greater than your assets). Ideally, as you approach middle age, you will have a *positive net worth*, meaning your assets exceed what you owe to others.

End Game Objective: Own, don't owe!

BANK

At businessdictionary.com, a bank is described as an establishment authorized by the government to hold money for businesses and individuals. Banks typically pay interest, clear checks, make loans, act as an intermediary in financial transactions, and provide other financial services to its customers.

BUSINESS BANK

A business bank is created for the purpose of focusing specifically on the needs of businesses and business owners. Its services are for business loans, lines of credit, and checking/savings accounts. It does not seek to service individuals or families.

COMMERCIAL BANK

A bank that provides its clientele with a wide range of services is a commercial bank. Checking and savings accounts, home and auto loans, safe deposit boxes, ATMs, and CDs are typical services offered in a commercial bank and available at one of its retail branches.

CREDIT UNION

An organization that offers services similar to a commercial bank but is a nonprofit owned by its members is a credit union. Rather than bank shareholders dividing up the bank's profits, the owner/members of a credit union share the profits among themselves.

Credit unions usually offer higher interest rates on certain types of accounts.

CHECKING ACCOUNT

A checking account is one of the main services offered in a bank. When you deposit your paycheck into a checking account, you can then distribute those funds to your creditors—the people, companies, and banks you owe or wish to give money to. Originally paid with numbered, handwritten paper checks, today's checking account funds can be paid through automatic bill paying programs (ACH) or through electronic fund transfer (EFT). Because most checking accounts do not earn interest, they should be used only for short-term deposits and payments.

SAVINGS ACCOUNT

A savings account is a good tool for accumulating funds for known expenses, such as home and vehicle maintenance as well as other defined purposes, such as vacations, home remodeling, and health-care deductibles. Savings accounts typically offer low interest rates and, therefore, should not be where the bulk of your assets are put.

 Twenty-five percent of American families have no savings at all.[6]

---

6 "American Family Financial Statistics," April 27, 2015. www.statisticbrain.com/american-family-financial-statistics.

INTEREST

Interest is the fee you pay to a bank or other lending institution to borrow their money; it also is what is paid to you for leaving your money in a bank account and allowing others to use your funds. When you are borrowing money, you look for a low interest rate (i.e., a low percentage of the total amount you are borrowing). When you are investing your money, you look for high interest rates (i.e., high percentages of your investment amount that will be paid to you).

SIMPLE INTEREST

Interest that is based on the principal—the dollar amount being borrowed or lent—is referred to as simple interest. Short-term loans—loans that will be repaid in a year or less—commonly use simple interest. With simple interest, you are not accruing or paying interest on any amount of money besides the initial principal. If you borrow $100,000 at a 5 percent interest rate and your loan is to be repaid over a ten-year period, you will eventually be paying $50,000 in interest in addition to your initial $100,000 principal—a total of $150,000. If you lent someone $100,000 ten years ago at a 5 percent interest rate, you will now be owed $150,000.

COMPOUND INTEREST

For longer-term loans, such as home mortgages or business loans, it is standard to apply compound interest, which, unlike simple interest, increases exponentially over time as interest payments are added to the original amount of the loan. As an easy example, you are going to borrow $1,000 at an interest rate of 10 percent, and you agree to repay the loan in ten years. In the first year, you will pay $100 in interest (10 percent of $1,000). That $100 will be added to your original $1,000, so that in the second year you will pay interest on $1,100, which is now $110, and so on for ten years. This compounding, or incremental increasing, can occur daily, monthly, quarterly, or annually, based on the terms of the loan, and will continue up to the tenth year when the entire loan is paid off. Now let's use the same scenario described under

> *Compound interest is the eighth wonder of the world. He who understands it, earns it... he who doesn't...pays it.*
>
> **—Albert Einstein**

Simple Interest above: If you borrow $100,000 and you are being charged an annually compounded interest rate of 5 percent, and you plan to repay the loan in ten years, you will ultimately pay $62,889.46 in interest. If you lent someone $100,000 ten years ago at 5 percent interest compounded annually, you will now be owed a total of $162,889.46. As you can see, when borrowing or lending money, it is essential that you have a thorough understanding of the terms of your loan.

SIMPLE VS. COMPOUNDED 5% INTEREST ON
$100,000 LOAN OVER 10 YEARS

Year	SIMPLE INTEREST Interest Paid Per Year	COMPOUNDED INTEREST Interest Paid Per Year
1	$5,000	$5,000.00
2	$5,000	$5,250.00
3	$5,000	$5,512.50
4	$5,000	$5,788.13
5	$5,000	$6,077.53
6	$5,000	$6,381.41
7	$5,000	$6,700.48
8	$5,000	$7,035.50
9	$5,000	$7,387.28
10	$5,000	$7,756.64
Total Interest Paid:	**$50,000**	**$62,889.46**

Savings with no compound interest

Savings with compound interest

ECONOMY

The economy of a wide geographic area, such as a country or region, is a broad term referring to its overall level of wealth and resources and its use and rate of production of goods and services. A strong economy is one in which business is active, manufacturing is productive, and people and companies are making and spending money at a healthy rate. A weak economy is one in which many people and businesses are under financial stress, there is a low rate of production of goods and services, and the overall population is less inclined to make purchases or invest in the future. The economic strength of a geographic area is always fluctuating and changing, creating different levels of supply and demand that impacts its overall financial picture.

INFLATION

Inflation refers to a general, steady increase in prices over a period of time, accompanied by a lowering of the purchasing power of money. Due to inflation in modern economy, $100 will not buy today what it could buy ten or twenty years ago. A certain level of inflation generally demonstrates a healthy economic picture. Inflation can reflect a good amount of demand for goods and services, and tied to that is a strong rate of employment.

INFLATION OR DEFLATION?

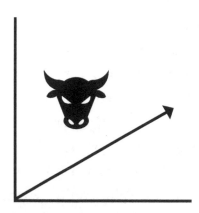 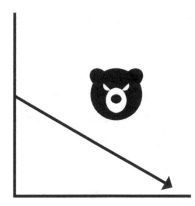

DEFLATION

Unlike inflation, deflation occurs when the prices of goods and services continue to fall. Chronic and widespread drops in prices are often a side effect of unemployment. Tied to unemployment is a decrease in both spending and demand for goods and service. These interlocking elements—drops in prices, growing unemployment, less demand for goods and services—can spiral into an economic depression.

ALPHABETICAL REFERENCE INDEX

A NOTE TO THE READER

The definitions above are intentionally concise and meant to be provided in general, easily understood terms. Each field of study or profession has its own uses and definitions of words, and those definitions are likely to be much more detailed and complex than those provided here. For additional and more comprehensive definitions, I recommend that you visit www.Dictionary.com, www.Investopedia.com, or my own website: www.navigatefinancialnw.com.

Positive: More in than out. You are living with the ability to not just survive but thrive.
Negative: Struggling, will crash eventually, without financial strength or resilience.

End Game Objective: Own, don't owe!

These are what you have to create the life you want, your flexibility, and your joy. Cash Flow and Net Worth are snap shots of your financial health and a reflection of your money attitude.

CHAPTER 3

YOUR CURRENT FINANCIAL PICTURE

*Before you can really start setting financial goals, you
need to determine where you stand financially.*

—David Bach, author of the *Finish Rich* book series

Now we come to a list of money-related questions, provided as a starting point to allow you to become more familiar with your finances. They are different from the questions in the first section in that those were focused on your attitudes and behaviors surrounding money, and these are specifically concerned with how much money you actually have at the moment. It will be helpful to keep in mind that while no one is expected to commit to memory all of the information these questions will

> *You can't be a big dreamer if you don't know where you are going. You can't know where you are going unless you first know where you are.*
>
> —Israelmore Ayivor,
> *Dream Big: See Your Bigger Picture!*

ask for, it is very much to your benefit to know where the answers can be found. If you are going to change your attitudes about money and take control of your finances, then you must have ready access to, and a clear understanding of, your own financial picture. Think of this exercise as a kind of **customized, financial GPS**; it's first going to show you where you are before telling you how to reach your destination. And don't we always need to know where we're starting from if we're serious about getting where we want to go?

Space is once again provided for you to make notes or actually record your answers.

- What is your monthly net income or take-home pay?

- Do you understand your payroll deductions?

- If you are self-employed, are you aware of your tax responsibilities?

- What are your assets? What do you own?

- Do you have debts (liabilities) that have not been paid or that you are currently paying off? How much do you owe and to whom?

- What is your net worth?

- What interest rates are you currently paying on your mortgage, car loan, credit cards, and other borrowed money?

- What interest rates are you earning in your various accounts (e.g., savings, checking, CDs, etc.)? Do the interest earned and the funds involved make financial sense?

- Do you generally have positive cash flow? At the end of the month, do you have money left over?

- Do you have a plan of action to pay off all your credit card balances every month? If not, why?

- Do you have a record of your financial interests stored in both paper and digital form in at least two different locations?

- List and briefly describe your monthly fixed costs and discretionary expenses.

- List your known expenses for the coming year, five years, ten years, and more.

- Do you regularly set money aside for these known expenses? How frequently do you add to those savings?

- Do you have an emergency fund? How many months' worth of overall living expenses are in it?

- Are you investing money? Have you reviewed your investments in the last six months? List the dollar amounts you have invested along with their corresponding investment vehicles.

- Do you have a retirement fund through your employer? Are you contributing the maximum amount allowed, and does your employer offer matching funds? What is the current size of your retirement fund?

- Take a look at your auto and home insurance policies to determine your coverage and deductibles. Do you have an umbrella policy, or excess liability policy, in place?

- Do you look at your bank statements each month? Do you understand the information provided? Have you been careful to discontinue automatic payments for services you are no longer using?

Some words of encouragement for those who are feeling overwhelmed after reading this list of questions:

1. If this feels completely daunting and outside of your capability, take a deep breath, take a few minutes, or take a walk. I assure you it is *not* outside your capability.

2. Start by targeting one question at a time. No one expects you to be able to gather all this information right away. Begin with just the questions that you automatically know the answers to without doing any research. Continue with those that can be answered by simply looking in files you have at home. Then try to schedule some time with people who can help (e.g., your human resources manager at work) for an explanation of your paycheck deductions.

3. Take it slow, and be thorough. Ignoring a tough question will neither make it go away nor make it any less important for you to understand.

My purpose in posing these questions is to motivate you to get organized so that you can become aware of what you have and understand what it means to have it. But remember, every journey starts with one step, and imagine how good it will feel once you have successfully tackled this chapter. You will then be in the very exciting position of preparing to move forward and building an intentional plan of action for your future!

The secret of getting ahead is getting started.

—Mark Twain, American author and humorist

CHAPTER 4

LIVING AND SPENDING WITH INTENTION

Any fool knows that to work hard at something you want
to accomplish is the only way to be happy. But beyond
that it is entirely up to you. You've got to do for yourself
all the seeking and finding concerned with what you want
to do. Anyone but yourself is useless to you there.

—Eugene O'Neill, American playwright

Actions come from decisions. Today's decisions affect tomorrow. Where you are today is a result of conscious and unconscious choices you've made in your life. And there is a ripple effect, too; choices you make impact others—even the small choices. We can never underestimate the far-reaching influence we can have, just by making our own decisions.

Several years ago, I had an idea for a day-long event for the women in my community. I saw women coming together, having fun, sharing knowledge, networking, growing, and—most importantly—feeling empowered. It took some time, but that initial vision went on to become a thought process, which became a decision, which led to an organizing committee, which ultimately produced exactly what I had envisioned. When the big day came, 200 women attended a conference where they made new connections, explored new opportunities, learned new skills, exchanged email addresses, and in some small (or big) way, changed the directions of their lives. This event has evolved and is still making an impact in my community today, even though I'm no longer directly involved. Today, there would be no way to begin to measure the sweeping impact of that one, inspired decision I made.

> *It is in your moments of decision that your destiny is shaped.*
>
> **—Tony Robbins**

It's even a decision whether or not to make a decision! Taking action or not is a choice. Every time you decide to attend a meeting, sign up for a class, reach out to a mentor, or simply ask a question, your decision will have some forward-moving effect on every aspect of your life and the lives of others. **Your options, your intentions, and ultimately, your legacy will be the result of the choices you make.**

Take a few moments and consider some decisions you have made and what they eventually led to. What is the *next* decision you will make?

WHERE ARE YOU GOING AND HOW ARE YOU GETTING THERE?

There are those who travel and those who are going somewhere. They are different, and yet they are the same. Successful people have this over their rivals: they know where they are going.

—Mark Caine, business author

Goals. Objectives. Mission. Purpose. Much has been written and spoken about on these subjects. Why? Because they are key to meeting our needs, realizing our potential, and achieving happiness. You really can't get there without them. Goals, by their very nature, involve a sense of purpose. Purpose and intention are consistent components in the lives of successful, fulfilled individuals. Once we recognize what our needs are, our purpose is to accumulate the knowledge and build the infrastructure we will require to achieve our goals and meet our needs.

As children, most of us are fortunate enough to have our needs met by the adults in our lives. As students and young adults, we have one main job and that is to recognize our talents and interest areas and figure out how to parlay them into marketable skill sets that will give us a lifetime of solutions for meeting our own needs. Once we arrive in the "real" world, however, life becomes complex, made up of entangled and often disconnected activities and conflicting personalities. We quickly learn to consider many different needs—those of our partners, children, parents, coworkers, bosses, neighbors, and scores of other people with whom we interact. How do we do it without losing our focus and sense of self? **We start by identifying the needs that must be met and then we establish goals that will enable us to meet them, and, finally, we make the intentional choice to take action.**

Invariably, some of those goals will contradict one another or, at best, not work congruently. When that happens, we find ourselves reacting to urgent situations, sudden opportunities, and new responsibilities. We try to be all and do all. Rather than remaining committed to our original tasks at hand, we quickly shift our focus and make decisions based on crises, compromises, and new sets of needs. Eventually, it all becomes confusing and uncomfortable. We feel disjointed and disconnected, frustrated and unfulfilled, scattered and stressed.

But if we have set our own primary goals based on our own *priorities and values,* and if we have built the infrastructure needed to address those goals, then we can avoid that voyage to burnout. **We will have a base to start from and a sense of purpose to guide us in the appropriate direction.** We will be working toward objectives that we created on purpose, with intention, and to meet very specific needs. The activities, challenges, and sacrifices along the way will be measurable against goals that are *meaningful to us.*

WHICH WOULD YOU PREFER?

Proactive

Helps protect you
from drowning.

Reactive

Thrown to you after
you're already drowning.

Research by many psychologists, and notably by Alexandra M. Freund and Marie Hennecke, in their paper, "On Means and Ends: The Role of Goal Focus in Successful Goal Pursuit," has demonstrated evidence that focusing on the process and the steps to reach the goal support goal achievement more than focusing on the outcome of the goal.

Your next question may be, *Where do those goals and guidelines come from? How do I arrive at those very specific priorities and construct a framework that will support them?*

My answer is to sit down with yourself and do a bit of reflection. Ask yourself these six questions:

1. What kind of person do I want be?

2. What do I need in my life in order to feel comfortable, satisfied, and worthy?

3. What kind of life shall I create that will address those basic needs?

4. What has prevented me from building that life in the past?

5. What am I willing to do without in order to have the life I want?

6. What steps can I take now, tomorrow, next week, next year, to directly or indirectly move closer to that life and to that person I want to be?

Here's an example, with answers provided by a friend and colleague who has recently retired and is now redesigning her life:

1. **What kind of person do I want be?** *I want to be a self-sufficient, self-directed, self-confident older person who is responsible, kind to others and the environment, and happy with my choices.*

2. **What do I need in my life in order to feel comfortable, satisfied, and worthy?** *I need a small, easy-to-maintain home that is safe, comfortable, and in good condition. I need things to do that will generate household income, speak to my creative spirit, contribute to my community, and give me the freedom and flexibility to enjoy my family, friends, and interests. I need to have simplicity and peace. I need to feel purposeful and successful in my activities and recognized and appreciated by others.*

3. **What kind of life shall I create that will address those basic needs?** *I will create a life built around who I am and what will work best for me. I will build an infrastructure of friends, family members, service providers, and other resources so that I have a safety net of support when I need it. I will seek opportunities to both create and teach art and to work as a writer and editor. I will remain engaged and*

involved with a number of outside activities and causes that are meaningful to me.

4. **What has prevented me from building that life in the past?** *In the past, I needed to work full-time and generate optimal income. I made a priority of trying to please others. I had aging parents for whom I was responsible. I lacked the self-confidence to express myself creatively.*

5. **What am I willing to do without in order to have the life I want?** *I am now willing to do without shopping sprees, unnecessary travel and entertainment, housecleaning and gardening help, a new car every few years, and the approval of most other people. Also, in order to rent out a room in my home for extra income, I am willing to do without complete privacy.*

6. **What steps can I take now, tomorrow, next week, next year, to directly or indirectly move closer to that life and to that person I want to be?** *I can re-invent myself as an artist and art instructor. I can reach out to the community and promote myself professionally, in both the art field and as a writer, editor, and proofreader. I can reduce spending to only basic necessities and occasional indulgences. I can take good care of my health, my home, and my attitude. I can remain creative and gradually teach myself new skills to broaden my marketability as an instructor.*

Then, make a list of things you are willing to accept. Here are some big ones to get you started:

- I am willing to accept this challenge, and I am willing to do the work.

- I am willing to consciously stop being all things to all people and instead, accept responsibility only for my own life.

- I am willing to do without some things in order to have the things that are truly important to me.

- Supplementing the items listed above, my newly retired friend added the following:

- I am willing to live a more casual and frugal life than I have been accustomed to until now.

- I am willing to go outside my comfort zone, break old bad habits and adopt healthy new ones, and let myself enjoy the new life I've designed for myself!

Everyone's answers will be, and should be, quite different. Whether you have a young family and your first priority is spending time with them, or you have kids applying for college and you must optimize your earnings, or you have a special penchant for nature and want to go live in the woods, all of your choices, activities, and sacrifices should get you closer to meeting those goals and aligning your life with those very personal values. There's a bonus waiting for you, too. **With this strong, well-defined purposefulness comes a sense of control over your own life that can be priceless.** It is a process and will take time. If you remain focused, you will prevail.

A word of caution: By now you may be doing some pretty intense emotional excavating, so be prepared. It is a powerful exercise. You will learn a lot about yourself. You will feel pride, and you may also feel disappointment. *Do not sink into depression because of all the things you haven't done and all the ways you haven't filled your potential.* Today is a new day, and your job is to stay focused now on your intentions as you move forward. "The first rule of personal finance," says James Altucher, successful entrepreneur and author of *The Choose Yourself Guide to Wealth*, "is that it's not personal and it's not financial. It's about your ability to make ten changes and not get too depressed over it."

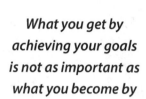

What you get by achieving your goals is not as important as what you become by achieving your goals.

—Henry David Thoreau, American author and philosopher

CLARIFYING YOUR FINANCIAL GOALS

To be in hell is to drift; to be in heaven is to steer.

—George Bernard Shaw, playwright

Think about tomorrow; chances are you will be there. If you start thinking about it now, particularly about how you would like your financial picture to look, regardless of how old you are now or how close to retirement, you will thank yourself when the time comes.

You must acquire the habits and skills of managing a small amount of money before you can have a large amount. Remember, we are creatures of habit and, therefore, the habit of managing your money is more important than the amount.

—T. Harv Eker, Canadian author, speaker, and businessman

Dr. Edwin Locke is an American psychologist and a pioneer in goal-setting theory. He conducted research that showed that the more difficult and specific a goal is, the harder people tend to work to achieve it. In one study, Locke found that 90 percent of the time, a goal that was challenging and specific but not overly challenging produced a higher level of output than a goal of "do your best." Having a goal that's too easy is not motivating. Difficult goals are more motivating than easy ones, because working hard for something leads to a greater sense of accomplishment.

To get started, identify your short- and long-term financial goals by actually writing them down. Consider putting them in a chart, at least three different milestones in each column, divided as follows:

Column 1: Six months from now

Column 2: One year from now

Column 3: Five years from now

Column 4: Ten years from now

For example, Ron and Jodi are young parents raising a growing family, with a combined take-home (net) income of $4,200 a month. Together, they've identified their core values, which include:

- A family life that is peaceful, satisfying, enriching, and based on mutual love, respect, consideration, and support

- Ongoing financial security for ourselves and our children

- Lives centered around responsible choices aimed at physical, emotional, and spiritual health

- Children being able to reach their potential and contribute to the world we live in

- A comfortable and secure retirement

Then, they might break down their financial goals as follows:

SIX MONTHS FROM NOW	ONE YEAR FROM NOW	FIVE YEARS FROM NOW	TEN YEARS FROM NOW
1. We will have established an emergency fund and have $1,000 in it.	1. We will have a total household emergency fund of $3,500.	1. Our emergency fund balance will have reached our goal of $12,600.	1. We will have had to access our emergency fund at least once or twice, and we will have replaced the funds we took.
2. We will have opened a "Put & Take" account and have a $600 balance.	2. We will have a balance of $1,200 in our "Put & Take" account.	2. We will have successfully used and replenished our "Put & Take" account fourteen times; account balance is now kept at $1,600.	2. We will have increased and maintained our "Put & Take" account balance at $2,200.
3. We will have paid off our credit card balance of $2,410 and maintained a balance of zero.	3. We will have started a college funding plan at $100/month.	3. We will have saved and fully paid for a trip to Disneyland.	3. Our children's college fund deposits are $400/month.
4. We will have increased our 401(K) contribution from 2 percent to 4 percent.	4. We will begin redirecting our "Put & Take" contributions to our emergency fund.	4. We are contributing $250 /mo. to our children's college fund.	4. We take a family vacation every year, which we save and pay for in advance.
	5. We continue to maintain our credit card balance at zero.	5. We have gradually increased both our 401(K) contributions to a total of 10 percent.	5. We're contributing the maximum 16 percent of our gross earnings to our 401(K) accounts.
		6. We continue to maintain our credit card balance at zero.	
		7. We will no longer be counting on each paycheck for survival.	

Try to align your actions with the results you desire. Ideally, each of the goals in these columns will reflect one or more of your answers to the questions you answered earlier.

As most of us know, life has a way of throwing an occasional curveball our way, despite our carefully laid out plans. A crumbling chimney, a flooded basement, a sudden health crisis, or a downturn in the economy can wreak havoc on your plans. Most likely, some of the goals you list in your chart will need to be adjusted over time. That said, however, try to commit yourself to achieving the three goals within each time period as closely as possible. If you amend your goals, be sure your reasons for doing so are good ones. A new hobby requiring the purchase of expensive equipment is not a good reason; the arrival of a new baby in the family is. By following your basic road map, you have less chance of getting lost on your way and a good chance of arriving where you want to be by the given time.

> *The goals you are defining and committing to will be challenging, but they are not impossible.*
>
> **—Dr. Edwin Locke,**
> **Toward a Theory of**
> **Task Motivation and**
> **Incentives, 1968**

TAKING RESPONSIBILITY

You are no longer a boy, and one of the first duties which a man owes to his friends and to society is to live within his income.
—Thomas Hughes, *Tom Brown at Oxford*

Making sound decisions is a critical skill that impacts every part of your life. Who you are, what you want, and how you intend to get it can involve hundreds or even thousands of important decisions facing you during your lifetime. It is part of being a responsible adult. We learn as adults to weigh the impact of our decisions on our own lives and those of others. Beginning with which college to attend and what subjects to study, through what career path will be rewarding, who is a good fit as a life partner, how large a family to have, and finally, when and how to retire, we each need to step up and take responsibility for ourselves. For some people, these kinds of choices can be excruciatingly difficult; in fact, many people will readily admit that they avoid making decisions—especially the bigger ones. They choose not to shape the direction of their own lives. They are living reactively and by default.

It is the same when it comes to managing finances. There are those who avoid financial activities or let their spouses handle money matters, dodging them until or unless they are forced to act. It can be a slippery slope, and I do not recommend it. I urge you to take responsibility for your own finances—even if you are in a long-term, committed partnership. You should always know what you have, where it is, what it is accomplishing for you, how you should and shouldn't spend it, and how to access major amounts should a need arise. Don't put it off.

In making financial decisions, there are some universal guidelines to consider as part of the process. Always be clear on your goals and objectives. Know where you're heading, what you need to accomplish, and what paths you should explore. Consider various approaches to achieving your goals. Perhaps there is no one right way. Be creative, yet logical. Be open-minded to new tools and techniques. Examine your alternatives with a critical eye. Looks for steps to improve or enhance the process. Find ways to build in flexibility, both for now and for the future. Think ahead.

Make decisions that make sense today but will also make sense many years down the road.

Years ago, I knew a couple who were remodeling their bathroom, including replacing the bathtub. Although it would cost more, they considered a new layout that would make the bathroom more accessible for people with physical mobility issues. Their intention was to still be living in the home for many more years. Once they began to age, the bathroom would have to accommodate their altered needs. They knew that remodeling costs were only going to increase, and if accessibility was important to them, then the best decision would be to take care of it now. Although they didn't need a wider bathroom now, it made sense for them to go ahead and spend the money rather than having to spend more of it in the future only to do the same thing. This was a good example of looking and thinking ahead to make a financial decision and having it pay off down the road—especially since they still live in the house and are now approaching their 70s!

Decisions need to be made consciously and intentionally, taking all possibilities into consideration. Focus on the impact the decision will have on all aspects of your life—cash flow, savings, relationships, individual and family health, time management, and other commitments. Living with intention is recognizing that the choices you make today are likely to touch all aspects of your life tomorrow.

MONEY AND THE CHOICES YOU MAKE WHEN PURCHASING

The amount of money you have has got nothing to do with what you earn. People earning a million dollars a year have no money. People earning $35,000 a year can be quite well off. It's not what you earn, it's what you spend.

—Paul Clitheroe, author of *Making Money,* and leading Australian financial planner

Money is a tool that can do one of two things. It can either be positioned to increase in value, or it can be spent. When you keep your money in a CD or an account where it is earning interest, or when you invest your money for the purpose of generating a profit in the future, you are positioning your funds to increase in value. When you make a purchase such as groceries, movie tickets, dinner out, or clothing, the funds are being spent. A vehicle is a purchase for which you will most likely never see those funds again, as are hedge trimmers, campers, treadmills, and patio sets. I encourage you to get in the habit of thinking before spending your money. Ask yourself these five questions:

1. What am I trying/hoping/going to accomplish with this purchase?

2. Do I already have anything else that can accomplish the same thing?

3. Will I use this item only on occasion or with some frequency?

4. Will this purchase help me achieve the larger goals I've set for myself?

5. If relevant, can I sustain/maintain this purchase?

I can't even remember all the shiny, new things I have considered buying in the past. I've had to ask myself what I would accomplish with an omelet pan … a garden edger … an electric ice cream maker … a new set of knives. The two truths I have learned as a result are (1) most purchases, while they would be nice or fun to own, will not move you any closer to meeting your personal goals; and (2) if you like it enough to consider purchasing it, *walk away from it,*

Time spent on personal tasks and on pleasure is how we spend an awful lot of our money. We can either devote less of our time to this to decrease our spending or we can find ways to maximize pleasure while minimizing our spending.

—Spending Time, Spending Money **by Trent Hamm**

and think about it overnight. If you sleep on it, still think the purchase is a good idea, and are certain it reflects your values and personal objectives, chances are it will still be there tomorrow.

In order to be independent and self-sustaining, you need to always be intentional about where you spend the money you worked hard to earn. Be sure you *need* the new camping tent and don't just *want* it. Can you rent or borrow one? Can you reserve a cabin instead? Will you use it enough for it to pay for itself? Do you go camping often, or is this a one-time opportunity? How often will you use a power washer, a rototiller, or a pasta attachment for your Kitchenaid? In fact, how often do you use the Kitchenaid? Feel good when you buy items by purchasing them with thought and purpose. Try to buy only those items that will benefit you over and over.

PRICE VS. VALUE

People do not always spend money wisely, because they cannot always accurately assess the opportunity costs associated with deferring a purchase or buying an alternative option.

—Erica Mina Okada and Stephen J. Hoch[7]

Price versus value should be an ongoing consideration when you are preparing to make a purchase. Determining value is an individual thing; what has value to someone else may seem unnecessary to you. Think of value as the return *you and your family* will get when using the product. You want to be sure you are indeed getting value and not just a low price. The two are often confused;

7　Erica Mina Okada and Stephen J. Hoch (2004), "Spending time versus spending money," Journal of Consumer Research, 31 (September), 313–323 many consumers believe if the price is low, then it must be a good value. If you find a great deal on a power tool, software program, or vehicle, it can be tempting. But if the tool on sale requires specialized bits or blades, then you may have just positioned yourself for higher operational costs. You may be better off spending more up front to save even more over time. If the software has all the bells and whistles you're looking for but they offer no tech support, how much extra will you have to spend for that? The minivan will certainly fit all your kids, but will the extra money you spend on gas be worth it? When you think about it, you see how it can be very expensive in the long run to not acknowledge the true cost of a purchase.

I have a car that I depend on for business, so a priority for me is that it be low maintenance and easy to repair. If a car is prone to breakdowns and requires expensive parts that are hard to find, it's not the right car for me. So when I bought it eight years ago, I was willing to spend a little more in order to have the car that would meet my needs—one that was known for long-term dependability and low maintenance. Being assured of those two things would have the greatest *value* for me. Now, fast forward to today. Eight years later, I've had a minimum of issues with the car, and my maintenance expenses have been consistently low. I've decided to keep the car for another three years. Even if I have to spend $3,000 a year in maintenance and upkeep, it will be far less expensive than purchasing a replacement vehicle. When I am ready to sell it, I'll have had the car paid for in full for many years. It will have been a great value, despite having to spend a little more on it initially.

I also own a truck. I use it, on average, only once or twice a month. It has value to me because it is convenient for hauling things, yard activities, and an occasional Saturday helping a friend move. It is not a necessity, nor do I need the world's most heavy-duty truck available. I spent very little to buy my truck, and I spend a minimum amount to maintain it. If I had to spend top dollar on repairs for it, I'd probably part with it, as it would then lose its value for me. I could replace it without having to spend very much, or I could easily rent a truck at an affordable rate for my actual "needs."

Here's one more example. Many growing families today purchase homes out in the country rather than closer to the core of their life's activities, because their dollar can buy a larger house with more land and lower taxes. While it is true their mortgage payments are lower, their overall living expenses are not. Factor in the combined costs of commuting, having larger rooms that need more heat and furniture and more acres that need mowing and landscaping, plus the hours of family time sacrificed, and it no longer seems like a great value.

As you can see, there is much to consider when determining value. I hope this will help you understand the thought process that should come before money and recognize that determining value has both objective and subjective components.

BREAKING BAD MONEY HABITS

We can never free ourselves from habit. But we can replace bad habits with good ones.

—Steven Pressfield, author

At a business conference a while back, a woman asked me, "How do I break the bad money habits I learned from my parents?" What a perceptive question! Not everyone realizes that the home where they were raised was often where they learned—or "inherited"—their habits and attitudes surrounding money.

As you know, habits are routine behaviors we repeat, usually without mindful consideration of the action. Some habits are good ones that support our quality of life (brushing our teeth, looking both ways at an intersection, thanking people when they hand us something, etc.). At times, they become so comfortable and routine, though, that they can lose their usefulness. How many times have you been driving somewhere over the weekend, and you suddenly realize that by not paying attention, you've gotten off the freeway at the exit you use on workdays?

Habits seldom develop in a vacuum; they frequently come from observing our parents. As a child, you believed—as most children do—that your parents were all-knowing and always right, so if they did it a certain way, that must have meant it was the *right* way. You grew up watching them, emulating them, copying them. The way you speak, the foods you eat, the holidays you celebrate, how you raise your children—all were modeled after what you saw in your home. The problem is that many of those habits you learned may not be *good* habits. But as habits, by definition, they tend to be our default behaviors, and changing them is undeniably challenging.

Let's go back to the woman at the conference. "Give me an example of a bad money habit you feel you learned from your parents," I said to her. "Easy," she replied. "My mother lived in avoidance and denial. She

> *The only proper way to eliminate bad habits is to replace them with good ones.*
>
> —Jerome Hines, author, *Four Voices of Man*

had such an aversion to paying bills that she let them pile up for several months at a time. Inevitably, it led to ridiculous late charges and credit issues accompanied by panic and blame between my parents. And even though I could see without question that it was not a good habit, I'm embarrassed to tell you I adopted it. Right now I have a stack of bills and overdue notices sitting on my desk!"

What should she do? One place to begin is by consciously reminding herself—and really believing—that her parents' habits *do not* have to remain *her* habits. She can repeat it to herself every day. No, she can never go back and change her parents' way of life, but she *can* be open to making adjustments in her own. She can develop a new habit of exploration, of keeping her eyes and ears open to how other people deal with monthly bill paying. She can ask a trusted friend or two to share their systems. What do they do with incoming mail? Where do they put the bills that need to be paid? Is there a certain day of the month they set aside for taking care of business? What do they do if they're short on cash? I believe that if she is motivated to break those habits, and if she has someone to model her new routines after, and if she knows the reward is far less stress and chaos in her life, *she can do it.*

Of course, it should be added that not all bad habits were learned during our youth. Suppose that until recently, you didn't

have a desk. Your bills and paperwork were scattered throughout the house, making it a challenge to locate them and get them all paid on time. But that was your routine. In fact, you did it for so long it felt comfortable. But one day you realized that if you simply created a dedicated space for your bills, you could take control over a destructive practice. With a new system and an intentional focus on your goals, you could develop some new, healthy habits around managing your finances. Then you found yourself a fun little basket to put on your desk and keep your bills all in one place. You then wrote a note in your planner to remind yourself on which day of the month your bills needed to be paid. Finally, you selected a small reward to treat yourself with after you successfully completed your task. You did this for three consecutive months and, by golly, you formed a new habit. Congratulations!

> "Friends greatly influence your choices. A 2014 study published in the *Journal of Consumer Research* found that friends often bond by providing one another with moral support to resist a temptation."[8]

For some people, professional assistance can be helpful in exploring and recognizing the behavioral triggers that keep them trapped within old habits that don't serve them well. It can be difficult to see those triggers ourselves, and support can make all the difference. Professional organizers and financial planners can also be helpful in gaining control, depending on the specific habits you want to break.

OVER-DESIRING OR WANTING IT ALL

We must consult our means rather than our wishes.

—George Washington

---

8 Amy Morin, "What Mentally Strong People Don't Do," Psychology Today. April 10, 2015.

You wander through the streets of an open-air art show as your eyes take in the vast array of artwork surrounding you. You already know you want the ceramic mug set, the hand-carved chopsticks, the framed photo of a French garden, and, of course, the silver puzzle bracelet. And you're only halfway through the fair vendors! Is this really why you came to the art show—to leave half the money you worked so hard for during the week? Or was it actually just to spend a pleasant day in the sunshine with friends, admiring beautiful things?

What happens to us when we find ourselves acting like irrational, childlike beings that want this, that, and everything else? We've all seen small children throw themselves on the floor when their parents won't buy them the toys they want. Is that what we've become? Is that really who we are? How do we control that gnawing desire to—simply put—have it all?

Over-desiring is not uncommon. Every one of us has our own weakness when it comes to wanting more, whether it is tools, car toys, clothing, shoes, jewelry, books, antique collectibles, or CDs. But there must be a way to handle that tendency to over-desire. How do you learn to use your internal "brakes" and stop the endless pursuit of more, more, more?

Between social pressure and global marketing masterminds, we are manipulated into wanting to have and experience all that we see and come in contact with. We go overboard buying consumer goods, we allow ourselves to depend on credit cards, and we continually search for the best new investment ideas that will make us rich so we can keep buying more. In today's world, it sometimes seems that there is no filter between desires and reason.

Although some social anthropologists might insist that over-desiring is as much a part of the human personality as fear, joy, and sadness, I believe that through mindful, intentional behavior we can overcome it and live in alignment with our core values. According to behaviorist and University of Missouri psychology professor Ian Zimmerman, "Impulse buying is related to anxiety and unhappiness, and controlling it could help improve your psychological well-being. To control something though, it's important to first understand it."[9] Dr. Zimmerman's writings propose that personality, pleasure, and product connections can all lead to impulse buys, and gaining an understanding of your personal triggers to these connections can help modify your motivation to participate in impulse buying.

Just recognizing the power that over-desiring can have on us is a good first step in being able to moderate and realign our energy and actions. Remind yourself often what your core values are. Believe in them. Commit yourself to them. Let them keep you centered and acting in moderation.

SAYING NO

You are only as rich as your will power.

—Wayne Chirisa, writer

The temptation to indulge is everywhere. It's on the phone asking you to meet for dinner and drinks. It's in the jewelry case at your favorite downtown boutique. It's in the showroom of the local car dealer, and it's waving at you from your TV screen, computer monitor, and every billboard along the highway. Sure, that cute sports car would make you feel good. Sure, it would be fun to meet for drinks. But saying yes all the time can also get you into

---

9   Ian Zimmerman, Ph.D, "Sold?" Psychology Today, July 18, 2012.

some serious trouble, with short- and long-term consequences you'd surely choose to avoid if you had it to do it over again.

What is it about saying no that turns us into overindulged children flailing on the floor of the toy store? Well, to start with, it means we have to deny ourselves those shiny new objects and once-in-a-lifetime opportunities that are sure to make us thin, popular, healthy, satisfied, and deliriously happy forever. Saying no makes us feel bad about ourselves. We pity ourselves and think we've let ourselves down. We should have stayed in school/kept that job/held on to those wedding gifts. Life isn't fair. Your neighbor has that lawn mower, so why can't you? And unfortunately, today's live-in-the-moment culture does not encourage prudent self-discipline when it comes to spending our money. We convince ourselves it'll be worth it! It's a chance we may never have again! Cost is secondary! Life's short, so *live* and *enjoy*! Right?

Wrong. Cost *does* matter, and there is a huge price to pay if we can't learn to simply say no.

> *Debt is like any other trap, easy enough to get into, but hard enough to get out of.*
>
> **—Henry Wheeler Shaw, 19th-century American humorist**

Each time you give in to instant gratification, you are affecting your financial security. Instead of saving, you are spending and racking up debt. Whether it is nickel-and-dime spending or big-ticket purchasing, you are pushing yourself away from your dreams. You'd be plenty annoyed if someone else purposefully kept you from those dreams, so why do it to yourself? Do you *want* to be one paycheck, one illness, or one crisis away from crashing? Doesn't a life built around your personal core values sound better and make more sense?

Most of us will live longer than our parents. So for many more years than we can even imagine, we will be dealing with both the short- and long-term consequences of our irresponsible, self-indulgent, over-desiring behaviors. Doesn't sound like fun to me. As mature adults, we know when we're not acting in our own best interests. No one needs to tell us when we're about to stray from an intentional thought process to an impulsive and reckless one. We know exactly what we're doing, and we're not fooling anyone—not even ourselves— not for a second.

Extreme emotions such as sadness and excitement impact impulse buying behavior. This is when we need to take a deep breath, step away from the whatever, and remember the big picture. If a purchase or dinner out doesn't directly get us closer to meeting our goals, we need to remind ourselves of the life we said we wanted and were committed to.

A CreditCards.com survey of 2014 reported that 28 percent of women and 14 percent of men participating in their survey made unplanned purchases when they were sad. On the opposite side of emotions, when excited, 50 percent of women and 47 percent of men have made impulse purchases.

Get back in touch with those core values again. Act in our own, true self-interest. **Be the grown-up in our relationship with ourselves.**

Here's another thought: If you can't walk through the mall without falling prey to the new spring fashions, don't go to the mall! If you can't say no when coworkers suggest lunch at the new bistro downtown, start to pack great lunches for yourself that will encourage you to eat in. If you get into trouble at outdoor art shows, enjoy the sunshine on a waterfront hike instead. Being intentional means being smart, sticking with your values, holding out for the greater prize.

Embrace your life, today and tomorrow. Make choices today you'll thank yourself for in the future. No one guarantees us a tomorrow, but if I *am* lucky enough to be here tomorrow, I want a life of my choosing. I want a life that reflects my goals and my values, one that allows me to feel secure and comfortable. I want to know that I have done all I can to sustain that life for myself and my family. To make that delicious thought a reality and to enjoy the priceless feeling of being financially grounded, I've trained myself to say no when I need to. I pass on opportunities to spend money and seek opportunities to spend time instead.

You can do this, too.

> *We make ourselves rich by making our wants few.*
>
> —Henry David Thoreau

SUPPORTING CAUSES YOU CARE ABOUT

Not surprisingly, many people who live their lives with intention and maintain a healthy money mind-set choose to become philanthropic and donate money to nonprofit organizations. This kind of involvement adds meaning and richness to our lives and demonstrates the very essence of purposefulness. "It feeds my soul," says one woman who supports a local domestic abuse shelter. "It gives me a purpose beyond my own life and needs," says an older gentleman who sends monthly checks to an animal rescue group.

In fact, a study conducted in 2009 by the National Institutes on Aging found that having a greater purpose in life is associated with living longer. "Our purpose is to be who we are," wrote author and relationship coach Cynthia Belmer in her 2014 book, *Meeting Freedom: How I let Go of Who I Thought I Should Be and Revealed My Authentic, Unstoppable Self.* "Our mission is to find something to live for."

As a charitable donor, you may find that your passion for the cause may fluctuate. But at those times in your life, whether you are financing your child's education, you've suddenly become a one-income household, or your business has taken a downturn, you don't have to abandon your cause. Instead, explore other ways to show support. Volunteering time for a project, procuring items for a fundraising auction, hosting a fundraising party in your home, or donating your professional services can be just as valuable to the organization and sometimes even a richer experience for you than writing a check.

Keep in mind also that the stronger your own finances are, the better you will be able to support groups and causes you care about. In the same way that

According to Dunn and Norton, authors of *Happy Money: The Science of Smarter Spending,* recent research on happiness suggests that the most satisfying way of using money is to invest in others. How you invest, how you participate in the "prosocial behavior" of investing in others can take many forms. However you choose to support nonprofit groups, for example, you are benefiting others and also achieving more personal satisfaction.

a flight attendant instructs us to first place the oxygen mask on ourselves before trying to assist others, it is best if you can give from a place of financial security, when you can be confident that your support is not jeopardizing your own future stability. If it means you need to step away for a while and direct your energies instead to building your career and increasing your income, that in itself is supporting the future of the organization. It is sad to say, but abuse, poverty, violence, and disease will still exist when you are in a stronger position to provide monetary support.

Issues dealing with career choices are hard to approach or address. Be open to exploring other ways to balance your passion with your financial responsibilities. If you have a limited income, your career choice may be serving your passion but stressing your ability to care for yourself or your family, today and into the future. Own the fact that you will have limited discretionary funds to spend on charitable donations. Accept your financial parameters, and rejoice in the service you're involved in. You can determine to change your career path to provide more financially, today and tomorrow, and still be involved with your passion in different ways for now, perhaps until the children are on their own or until you're retired. You have a continuum of choices; it's not 100 percent one or the other.

Finally, although many new charitable donors aren't aware of them, there are numerous giving programs available that will allow you to support a non profit while also generating income for yourself. Most financial advisors and estate attorneys are well versed in what those charitable giving tools are and can direct you to the ones that make the most sense for you.

Those of us in a position to give to causes we care about are indeed blessed. For a purposeful, passionate, and meaningful life, I wholeheartedly recommend it!

CHAPTER 5

PLANNING WELL, LIVING WELL

Women who have it all should try having nothing: I have no husband, no children, no real estate, no stocks, no bonds, no investments, no 401(k), no CDs, no IRAs, no emergency fund—I don't even have a savings account. It's not that I have not planned for the future; I have not planned for the present.

—Elizabeth Wurtzel, author *Prozac Nation*

I used to belong to a monthly business networking group in my community, where we would take turns giving our names and elevator speeches—you know, those concise, 15-second "commercials" we would recite if we had just 15 seconds to ride in the elevator with a potential client. Each group member was encouraged to come up with her own elevator speech and practice it at our networking meetings. Mine fit the bill—it was short and covered the most important points about the benefits of financial planning. But it was my tagline that really resonated with the other members. Each month, at the end of my elevator speech, I would pause momentarily and then conclude with my tagline—

"People don't *plan to fail*; they *FAIL TO PLAN*"—as everyone else in the room recited it out loud along with me. I loved that my words made such an impression!

To start this chapter, therefore, I will borrow my own tagline, because for a chapter about the benefits of planning your finances, I couldn't find a better way to begin. Nor can I think of any singular point I would want you to remember from this book more than the critical importance of *planning when it comes to your money*. With our lives as busy and full as they are, with multitudes of responsibilities and things to remember, we can do ourselves no greater favor than making sure we have a proactive and protective blueprint concerning our money.

The premise that good self-control is central to success across life domains, from school to work to relationships is a given in Michael Inzlicht, University of Toronto, Department of Psychology paper, "Exploring the Mechanisms of Self-Control Improvement," written with Lisa Legault and Rimma Teper, who are also academics of psychology. Key elements of their work is the importance of emotional acceptance in goal monitoring, conflict detection, and intentions on implementing behavioral changes.[10]

You've decided to take a leave from your job and attend

When you establish a destination by defining what you want, then take physical action by making choices that move you towards that destination, the possibility for success is limitless and arrival at the destination is inevitable.

—Steve Maraboli, *Life, the Truth, and Being Free*

---

10 Current Directions in Psychological Science, August 1, 2014.

graduate school. What's your plan? You're buying a house that needs major renovations. A new baby is on the way. An earthquake hits and puts you out of business. You and your spouse want to travel the world when you retire. What's your plan?

The *2012 Household Financial Planning Survey* published by the CERTIFIED FINANCIAL PLANNER™ Board revealed a startling statistic: In the United States, fewer than one-third of all household decision makers are participating in any long-term financial planning activities, either with professional support or on their own. Further, according to a survey conducted in 2013 by Bankrate.com, a personal finance website, more than 75 percent of Americans don't have enough money saved to pay their bills for six months—and possibly as many as half could only cover their expenses for three months or less. Most alarming, more than one-quarter of Bankrate's survey respondents admit to having no reserves to draw on in the event of an emergency.

> 27 percent say they have less than $1,000 in savings (up from 20 percent in 2009). In total, more than half of workers (54 percent) report that the total value of their household's savings and investments, excluding the value of their primary home and any defined benefit plans, is less than $25,000.[11]

I cannot stress enough the importance of planning ahead financially. Planning ahead helps us to navigate through the changing needs and stages of our lives and gives us options and flexibility to cushion us during tough times. It can position us to act ahead of the situation and purposefully take action from a place of strength and control rather than from vulnerability and panic. Our overall

---

11 Retirement Confidence Survey, 2012

comfort and security in our later years will have a direct proportion to the amount of financial planning we do now. Again, it's all part of that purposeful, responsible mind-set we've committed ourselves to. Be prepared and have a plan, or scramble around afterward and wonder what happened. You know which one I'd pick.

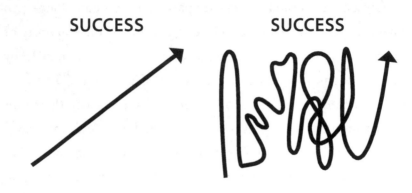

SUCCESS	**SUCCESS**
What people think it looks like	What it really looks like

Financial Success	**Financial Success**
A. Earn a good living	A. Don't earn enough, then spend too much; Make mistakes, learn from them; Manage your income and expense.
B. Get in a Relationship	B. Hide or misrepresent earnings or spending behavior; Work against each other's emotions and values; Struggle with communication about money and the impact of individual/joint decisions; Start talking and owning behavior and the impact of decisions; Work with your significant other and family to achieve your goals.

What people think it looks like	What it really looks like
## Financial Success	## Financial Success

C. Take out a mortgage on a house, buy another, then another

C. Buy a house without a strong down payment or realizing the incidental costs; Buy up and take on a larger mortgage; Recognize a home is a constant and needs to be affordable in every way, short term and long term; Strive to maintain and own the house that supports your long term and short term goals.

D. Buy a car, the most expensive one you can afford

D. Buy the car of your dreams, even if it costs more than you can pay for and cover all your other expenses; Major car repair and you cannot make the payments and fix the car; Use credit cards to cover the repairs; Three years later you are still paying the debt; Car is paid off, you keep it for three more years, start to save to buy an affordable car; Buy a car, pay it off, and maintain for longevity.

E. Retire

E. Live paycheck to paycheck, everytime you try to save you end up spending it; You have started to save regularly and you have been able to maintain a strong balance for years. You no longer maintain a credit card balance; You start saving with your employers 401K, scared you're saving too much and not enough; You increase your savings with every raise and cost of living increase, you have maxed out your contribution limit for your Roth and 401K; Your house is paid off before you retire; Retire with dignity and resources.

CASH FLOW

Frugality includes all the other virtues.

—Cicero

Cash flow is the foundation of all your financial decisions, your means for feeding, housing, and clothing yourself and your family, the protective armor you wear in anticipation of life's occasional surprises. The hard truth is that many of us spend more than we earn—or come awfully close. Your cash flow, which is essentially the money coming in and going out, is the baseline you count on weekly, monthly, annually, throughout your life, to be able to remain safe, secure, and comfortable and, hopefully, to have a little fun with as well. **It's the ultimate survival tool—with perks.**

Money is a somewhat or very significant source of stress for the majority of Americans (64 percent) but even more so for parents (77 percent), millennials (75 percent), and Gen Xers (76 percent).[12]

Money, like emotions, is something you must control to keep your life on the right track.

—Natasha Munson, Life Lessons for My Sisters: How to Make Wise Choices and Live a Life You Love!

The place to begin in managing your cash flow is a two-step process. First, know how much money is coming into and going out of your household on a regular basis. Make every effort to understand your paycheck, mortgage agreement, insurance policies, and 401(K). Keep track of all *unearned income* as well, such as

---

12 "Stress in America™ survey," American Psychological Association, 2014.

the money you get for renting out a garage space or your monthly pension checks.

Have a realistic idea of how much you have to work with, and then put it to work, using it as needed and desired to live the life you want.

As we've talked about in previous sections, the extent to which you have defined your life goals and identified your core values will have a direct impact on how effectively you make your cash flow work for you.

FIXED EXPENSES

These continuous regular expenses simply fill up our budget, leaving us less money to invest for the future—and also less money to spend on things that we enjoy.

—Trent Hamm, writer for SimpleDollar.com

When figuring out your cash flow, you will factor in not only the money that is coming in but also how much is going out. Your fixed monthly expenses are the first to consider, as they are predictably constant and have little or no fluctuation. Examples are your rent or mortgage payments, utilities, insurance premiums, loan installments, homeowners' association fees, monthly housecleaning and/or landscaping services, club dues, and gym memberships.

Heavy fixed expenses can sometimes make us feel trapped and overwhelmed, so be sure that what you are spending your hard-earned cash on is paying off for you. Don't spend more than is needed to maintain your life. The more you can minimize your fixed expenses, the more you will have left for unanticipated expenses—and you *will* have them—as well as more discretionary spending—and savings, of course.

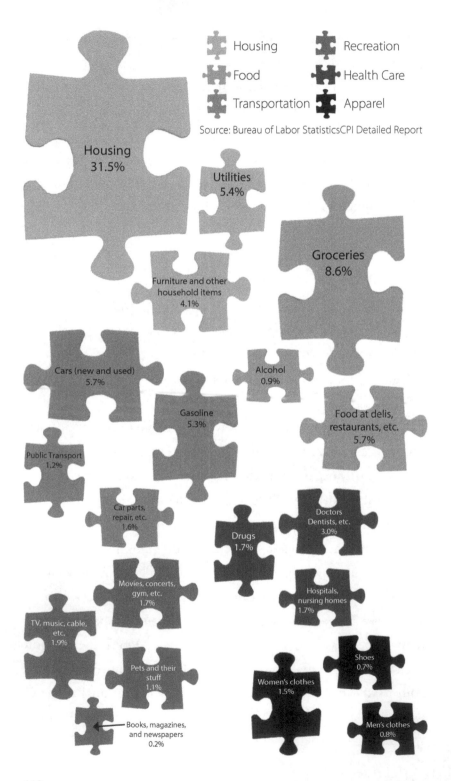

Housing   Recreation

Food   Health Care

Transportation   Apparel

Source: Bureau of Labor StatisticsCPI Detailed Report

Housing
31.5%

Utilities
5.4%

Groceries
8.6%

Furniture and other
household items
4.1%

Cars (new and used)
5.7%

Alcohol
0.9%

Gasoline
5.3%

Food at delis,
restaurants, etc.
5.7%

Public Transport
1.2%

Car parts,
repair, etc.
1.6%

Drugs
1.7%

Doctors
Dentists, etc.
3.0%

Movies, concerts,
gym, etc.
1.7%

Hospitals,
nursing homes
1.7%

TV, music, cable,
etc.
1.9%

Shoes
0.7%

Pets and their
stuff
1.1%

Women's clothes
1.5%

Books, magazines,
and newspapers
0.2%

Men's clothes
0.8%

In recent years, the median American monthly income has been $4,000, 80 percent of which goes toward regular monthly expenses like groceries, housing, gasoline, insurance, and the like.[13]

And while there are always going to be some fixed expenses you cannot adjust, I recommend that you look at your fixed costs closely and with a critical eye. There are usually ways you can cut corners without it hurting too much. Keep in mind, for example, that insurance premiums are often less expensive if paid annually instead of monthly. If you're primarily using your mobile phone, you may be able to get by without a landline. (A friend of mine saved $65 monthly by discontinuing her home phone account.) Yes, it takes focus and discipline to hold on to those funds over a year's time, but it can be very cost effective for you.

A final word about fixed expenses: What may seem like relatively small monthly payments—such as gym memberships and loaded cable TV deals—have a way of adding up pretty quickly. Are you actually going to the gym and taking full advantage of all your cable channels? Aside from being sure you have the best possible deal on your cable package, think about going a month or two without it and seeing how much

> *Good habits, which bring our lower passions and appetites under automatic control, leave our natures free to explore the larger experiences of life. Too many of us divide and dissipate our energies in debating actions which should be taken for granted.*
>
> **—Ralph W. Sockman, author**

---

13 Naomi Mannino, "Scary: Americans Saving Less Than $100 a Month," July 3, 2013.

it is missed. Are there other things you're paying for—or paying more for—than you need to? Be a detective and challenge yourself to see what you can dig up.

EXPECTED EXPENSES

Some expenses are typically paid on an annual basis. Your kids' soccer memberships and gymnastics tuition are examples, as is your dog's annual visit to the vet. The costs of home and automobile maintenance also fall into the category of expected expenses. After all, needing a new stove or set of brakes is not an "if" situation—it's a "when." We know those expenses are coming up, yet when the time comes, we're not prepared, and we have to find other ways of covering them. Too often, individuals and families respond to these events as if they were an emergency. They'll find it tempting to pay for them out of their retirement savings or put them on a credit card or even liquidate a small CD.

I have a useful approach I'd like to recommend. Sit down and look at what you spent last year on all these expected expenses. Add them up, build in an extra amount as a small cushion, and divide by 12. Consider this a new fixed, monthly expense that is **as meaningful and important as your mortgage payment**. Write yourself a monthly check, and deposit it into an easily accessible account or, better yet, set up auto deposits. It may take a year or more to get this new, proactive system up and running, but when you do, you will reap the rewards. You will now be able to better enjoy your discretionary spending without being concerned that you are dipping into funds meant for other obligations. You also will be glad when your credit card bill comes and it's not loaded with expenses you can't cover right away and will ultimately pay steep finance charges on.

Another system of which I am a huge fan is maintaining what I call a "Put & Take" account at a local bank. If you consistently keep $800 to $2,400 in this type of account, the funds will be there to cover those inevitable expenses. When you utilize those funds to buy a new set of brakes or replace your stove, you will be less strapped and far less stressed. Then—*and here's the very important part*—be sure that over the next few months you replenish those funds until your account balance is back where it was before you took the money out. We'll talk more about the "Put & Take" idea later on when we cover emergencies and how to survive them.

The best systems take time, focus, and forethought, but having these reserves and continuing this pattern of proactive activities will go a long way in keeping you calm and your finances stable.

VARIABLE EXPENSES

Additional expenses to include in your "money going out" category are those that you generally pay on a monthly basis but are not necessarily the same each month. In fact, the amounts you pay can fluctuate greatly from one month to the next. Good examples of those *variable expenses* are your food, gas, clothing, healthcare, and gifts. You spend less on gas in the winter than you do in the summer, when you take road trips most weekends. You spend more on groceries and gifts in December, when your family comes to town for the holidays. Clothes shopping may be a big expense in September if you're sending children back to school, but in the hot summer months, you seldom shop for clothing. While these are expenses most of us have to include in our outgoing funds, we do have choices, and if we want to cut down on these and look hard enough, we'll often find numerous ways to cut back. Explore destinations for your weekend road trips that are closer to home, or limit road trips to just twice monthly. Make use of price reductions throughout the year, and store food in your freezer to keep holiday expenses from breaking the bank. And if you wait for seasonal markdowns or shop in outlet stores, you can purchase back-to-school wardrobes for far less than retail prices. These kinds of short-term choices can have long-term impact and leave you more to play with.

DISCRETIONARY SPENDING

"We have become a society of indulgent consumers resulting in rapidly increasing debt both personally and as a nation."

—L.G. Durand, nonfiction author and publisher

As the proverb says, "All work and no play makes Jack a dull boy." In our own lives, it means what we all know to be true, that without time off from work, we can become both bored and boring. Add those two together and you've seriously compromised your quality of life. Does this mean you should drop everything and head for Disneyland? Throw caution to the wind and buy the kayak you've always wanted? Of course not, but you can—and should—allow for some funds in your spending that will cover activities that you know will enhance and enrich your life.

Here, again, you have the ability to control how much and how often you make these discretionary purchases. Rather than looking for a brand new kayak, search the Internet for a gently used one. Perhaps a nearby theme park would fit the bill as much as a costlier trip to Disneyland would have. I don't believe you need to sacrifice all dinners out and theater tickets for a year in order to live with intention, but you needn't go the most expensive route, either. Controlling what you can, remaining flexible, and keeping an open mind when it comes to entertainment and luxuries will help you avoid sabotaging your financial goals in the name of fun and stress relief.

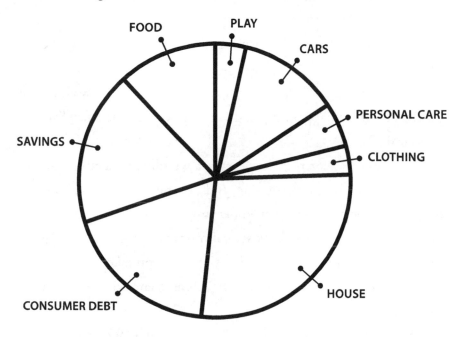

WHAT DOES YOUR PIE CHART LOOK LIKE?

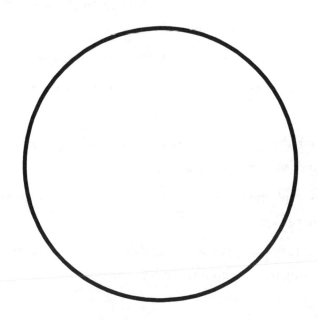

WHEN IS IT AN EMERGENCY AND HOW CAN YOU BE PREPARED FOR IT?

Wisdom from My Parents

From my mother: "It wasn't raining when Noah built the Ark."

From my father: "The spare tire is always inflated and waiting for the flat tire to happen. If you drive, you will change a few flats in your life."

Everyone has emergencies. They're a weirdly predictable, and sometimes unpleasant, part of life, and no one gets away without them. You, or someone you know, might have lived through terrible crises that set you back several months or even came close to wiping out your savings. So what steps can you take now to be prepared for those inevitable and unavoidable emergencies when they occur?

First, let's establish when it *isn't* an emergency. We've already decided it *isn't* an emergency when your brakes need replacing or your stove dies. Your "Put & Take" account is there for just that purpose. It also *isn't* an emergency when:

- you have a prescription requiring new eyeglasses,

- your son's class goes on an educational overnight field trip,

- your daughter learns that she needs to purchase an expensive bridesmaid dress,

- your phone company comes out with an updated smartphone,

- you have your eye on a beautiful piece of art but are not getting paid for another two weeks,

- the summer heat is unbearable and your air conditioning has broken down,

- there's a sale on computers and yours is on its last breath,

- and so on.

You get the picture. And you don't want to give in to the temptation of putting all these "would-be-nice-to-have" purchases on your credit card. Paying outrageous finance charges when you can't take care of your balance in a month is obviously going to add costs on to your original purchase. Once again, at the risk of being repetitive, these purchases are what your "Put & Take" account is for—but only if you know you will be able to replace those funds within one or two months!

On the other hand, it *is* considered an emergency when:

- you are in a collision accident and have a deductible to pay,

- your mother has fallen ill, and you must travel across the country to be with her,

- a tree on your property falls over and crushes your neighbor's only car,

- your partner urgently needs non-elective surgery, and you anticipate a huge hospital bill,

- an injury keeps you out of work, and your income disappears,

- your child gets badly hurt at day camp, and you must immediately hire legal counsel,

- or damage from an earthquake is forcing you to move into a motel indefinitely.

Again, you get it. These are real emergencies. I know families who have dealt with every example on this list … and then some. Although most are not true life-and-death scenarios, they are potentially huge expenses about which *you do not have a choice*. They can do major damage to your savings in no time. They can set you back, delay your retirement, and leave you in debt for many years to come.

The solution in these types of cases is an *emergency fund*. Your emergency fund should be equal to the total amount of your fixed expenses for a period of no less than three months. If you spend $2,000 a month on your mortgage and all your bills and day-to-day costs, you should have (i.e., *it would be in your own best interest to have*) about $6,000 in an emergency account. If your expenses are $3,200 then you need to have $9,600 in an emergency account. Talk to someone at your bank about putting it in an interest-bearing account where it can earn interest and add to the dollar amount you have in there.

Right about now, I bet you're thinking I'm asking too much, going overboard, not being realistic, assuming everyone's got a paycheck that will stretch that far. You're questioning whether other people have actually set aside this kind of crisis money. *Besides,* you're thinking, *I have a nice cushion of $800 to $2,400 in my "Put & Take" account, and I'm already holding on to other money for my first-of-the-year financial obligations. Where am I supposed to find another $6,000 to establish an emergency fund?*

A few years ago, Jessica Dickler from CNNMoney.com figured that 65 percent of Americans do *not* have at least $1,000 to cover unexpected emergency expenses. When a need arises, Dickler reported, they borrow money from family members or put extraordinarily large amounts on credit cards.

You do not have to leave yourself in that vulnerable position. You won't have to regret not being more careful in order to live the life you've chosen for yourself. And later on in your life, you can grow older in comfort and security. If you can spend a few years *now* to be in that enviable position, would you?

THE BIG PICTURE

I know a couple who, in order to save money, decided to sell their spacious home in the suburbs when their youngest child left for college. They looked forward to buying a smaller, nicely appointed condo in the city where all the chores, such as mowing, weeding, painting, hedge trimming, window washing, snow shoveling, and leaf raking, would be taken care of for them. Ongoing home maintenance would no longer cut into their recreational time or have to be paid for when they chose not to do it themselves. A closer proximity to entertainment, restaurants, and galleries, not to mention their workplaces, was also a big consideration for them. They were sure they'd save a ton of money, especially on gas.

Their big surprises came when they finally made the move. It turned out that their two spaces in the parking garage cost more than the gas they had been pumping into their cars. Their membership in the gym downstairs was a pricey extra expense they also had not considered, but with all their newfound extra time, it made sense for them to join. Their large-scale furniture now looked out of place in their cozy condo, requiring some extensive furniture shopping. But perhaps their biggest bombshell was how easily they gave in to the temptations all around them. Movie and theater tickets and dinners out several times a week added up much more quickly than they counted on.

Had my friends looked at the big picture and factored in the costs associated with an urban lifestyle, they would have been prepared for the shock. They also would have seen that their projected savings were unlikely to appear any time soon.

I hope you'll remember my friends' story, and look at the big picture before making critical financial decisions! Avoid sabotaging your well-intentioned money management efforts by knowing what your priorities are and what they're going to cost you before committing yourself to a budget.

That said, I will also add that budgets are never written in stone. They are guidelines that should give you some built-in flexibility for when life happens and you need some extra resources. But if you let it, **your budget will provide prudent and responsible parameters for living within your means**, offering you a better-than-reasonable chance of being successful in achieving what you've set out to. After all, a goal without resources is but a dream; a goal with resources can eventually become your new reality.

One final thought regarding budgeting: Consider embracing the shared mind-set of people who manage their finances with intention and live within your means! Set up your budget to spend *less* than what you earn. In my practice, I still see too many people needlessly placing themselves in financial tight spots by living as though they expected sudden windfalls to show up and rescue them. Even just one or two mini-catastrophes and their lives could come tumbling down. I'm not encouraging you to live in a tepee in the woods or deny yourself a movie on occasion, but I am saying, "Be realistic!" Set yourself up for success and satisfaction rather than failure and frustration.

THE B-WORD

By now you know that analyzing your goals and visions for your life, and prioritizing them, and then allocating the resources necessary for their attainment is the root of financial management. Having and sticking to a *budget* will be key to making this process work for you. It will be the basic foundation for assigning your resources and allocating your funds. And yet, many people do not include budgeting as part of their money management strategies. They avoid living within a budget as though it were an inescapable prison that will deny them freedom and deprive them of fresh air.

A carefully developed budget provides us with an intentional, reliable framework for creating and maintaining financial sustainability. It helps us plan for anticipated expenses and prepare for the unanticipated ones. A budget allows us to keep our commitment to our goals and financial well-being by predetermining our parameters for all our expenditures.

As a financial planner, I meet far too many individuals who have never drawn up a budget, who spend money today but don't consider what they will need tomorrow. Money seems to burn holes in their pockets; if they have it, they feel they can spend it. They purchase everything from cruises and concert tickets to jigsaws and jewelry and too easily "forget" that they have a big insurance premium or credit card bill coming up. They don't see how a budget will help them exercise more control, recognize their parameters, avoid impulsive spending, and escape the unpleasant surprises that follow. I believe that with an effective personal budgeting system, they could achieve a level of financial stability and flexibility that will support their overall life plan. For those who need it—and there are many—it would help to curb their natural tendencies to give in to their desires and act irresponsibly.

A budget would allow them to see the path that is ahead of them and be ready to follow it.

And if those reasons aren't enough, here's one more: a budget would **help them sleep better at night.** Nearly 80 percent of more than 2,100 people admitted that their personal finances keep them awake at night.[14]

Whenever I'm asked for the ideal time to draft or develop a budget, I have a stock answer: ASAP. If you don't have one, come up with one. Logically, a budget is better when it's written down. When we can see it, when it's in front of us, it seems to make it more real. It allows us to recognize when and where adjustments need to be made and gives us a tangible tool for comparing how we're doing this month/year to how we did last month/year.

Seventy-one percent of consumers admitted to having personal finance worries with not enough savings, job issues, debt, and credit topping the list. That survey was conducted in March 2014, by Harris Poll among 2,016 Americans aged 18 and older.

As we know, life changes, and circumstances change. Sometimes for the better, sometimes not. When it happens, you will want to update and adjust your budget. Tax time is also a good opportunity to make adjustments, as you will then have a realistic number that represents your earnings from the past year, which will usually be a good indicator of what they will be in the coming year.

If I've convinced you, I'm glad, and I congratulate you on a responsible decision! Now, I don't want you to be frightened to do this. It's not very daunting, really. It needn't be a lengthy, formal, or complicated document; a plain piece of paper and pen

---

14 National Foundation of Credit Counseling Financial Literacy Opinion Index, July 2014

or pencil are all you need to start. In a while, you will need your checkbook registers or bank transactions from the past six months to a year so you can see realistically what you've been spending up until now, so you can more easily estimate what you'll need for the time that's ahead.

BUDGET TEMPLATE #1

Fixed Monthly Expenses	Planned	Actual	Difference/Rolling Bal
Mortgage/Rent Payment			
2nd Mortgage/HELOC			
Auto Loan			
Personal Loan			
Credit Card Payments			
Home/Renters Insurance			
Auto Insurance			
Life Insurance			
Disability Insurance			
Long-term Care Ins.			
Health Insurance			
Umbrella Liability Ins.			
Total Fixed Expense:			

Fixed Monthly Expenses	Planned	Actual	Difference/Rolling Bal
Gas			
Electricity			
Water/Sewer			
Cable/Satellite TV			
Telephone			
Cell Phone			
Food			
Clothing			
Dry Cleaning/Laundry			
Child Care			
Personal Care			
Home Repairs/Maint.			
Home Improvements			
Auto Gas/Oil			
Auto Repairs			
Educational Expenses			
Entertainment/Dining			
Club/Association Dues			
Gifts/Donations			
Recreation/Travel			
Hobbies			
Unreimbursed Medical/Dental			
Miscellaneous/Cash			
Total Fixed Expense:			

Net Cash Flow	Current
Take Home Monthly Income	
Total Fixed Expenses	
Total Variable Expenses	
Discretionary Income (Income - Expenses)	

BUDGET TEMPLATE #2

INCOME — MONTHLY BUDGET AMOUNT

Category	Planned	Actual
Employment Income #1		
Employment Income #2		
Other Income		

EXPENSES — MONTHLY BUDGET AMOUNT
1. Home Expense

Category	Planned	Actual
Mortgage/Rent		
2nd Mortgage/HELOC		
Real Estate Taxes		
Homeowner Insurance		
Homeowner Dues/Assn Fees		
Electricity		
Gas		
Water/Sewer		
Garbage Collection		
Cable/Satellite TV		
Telephone		
Internet		
Home Repairs/Maint.		
Major Home Repairs/Remodel		
Furniture/Household Items		
Miscellaneous		

EXPENSES — MONTHLY BUDGET AMOUNT
2. Automobile Expenses

Category	Planned	Actual
Loan/Lease Payment		
Loan/Lease Payment #2		
Auto Insurance		
Vehicle Licensing		
Auto Maintenance/Repairs		
Fuel		
Parking/Tolls		
Miscellaneous		

EXPENSES — MONTHLY BUDGET AMOUNT
3. Liabilities

Category	Planned	Actual
Credit Card Debt		
Credit Card Debt		
Credit Card Debt		
Credit Card Debt		
Student Loan Payment		
Personal Loan Payment		

EXPENSES — MONTHLY BUDGET AMOUNT
4. Personal Expenses

Category	Planned	Actual
Groceries		
Entertainment/Dining		
Clothing		
Personal Care		
Pet Care		
Dry Cleaning/Laundry		
Gifts		
Charitable Donations		
Child Sports/Activities		
Child Allowance		
Child Tutor		
Recreation		
Vacation/Travel		
Cash/Miscellaneous		

EXPENSES — MONTHLY BUDGET AMOUNT
5. Personal Insurances

Category	Planned	Actual
Life Insurance		
Disability Insurance		
Long-term Care Ins.		
Medical Insurance		
Umbrella Liability Ins.		
Other		

EXPENSES — MONTHLY BUDGET AMOUNT
6. UnReimbursed Medical Expenses

Category	Planned	Actual
Medical Expenses		
Dental Expenses		
Vision Expenses		
Prescription Expenses		

BUDGET TEMPLATE #3

LIVING EXPENSES	TYPE OF EXPENSE		AMOUNT OF EXPENSE	
	Discretionary	Fixed	Monthly	Annual
Auto Gas/Repairs				
Auto Insurance				
Auto Loan/Lease				
Cash				
Charity/Donations				
Child Care				
Clothing				
Dining/Entertainment				
Disability Insurance				
Furniture/Household Items				
Gifts				
Groceries				
Hobbies				
Home Repairs/Maintenance				
Homeowners Insurance				
Life Insurance				
Medical Insurance				
Membership Dues/Fees				
Pet Care				
Property Taxes				
Tuition/Books				
Umbrella/Liability Insurance				
Utilities				
Vacation/Travel				

Of the two primary components of a budget, the first to be considered is your income. Your take-home pay is fairly easy to determine since it is often fixed, meaning it doesn't vary much from one month to the next—similar to your fixed expenses described earlier. Occasional fluctuations, such as a raise due to a promotion, or a Cost of Living Allowance (COLA), will cause your paycheck to go up slightly every January, and you can factor that into your budget each year. Of course, if you are self-employed, work on commission, or do mainly seasonal work, your monthly income will fluctuate, but you can most likely predict what you will bring in based on your income in previous years. In any case, when figuring out your income for budgeting purposes, be conservative, as it will build in a level of flexibility you will come to appreciate.

Your anticipated monthly expenses are the other major component of your budget. You will need to make a list of them, beginning with your fixed expenses. Those include your mortgage or rent payment, car and other loan payments, insurance premiums, utilities, memberships—whatever expenses you have that are the most unchanging on a month-to-month basis. Next to the descriptions of the expenses, e.g., house payment, auto loan, etc., write down what you spend monthly for each thing. House payment: $1,100. Auto loan: $225. College loan: $62. Utilities: $140, and so on. (If you're not on a budget plan with your utilities company, in which you pay the same amount every month based on the previous year's consumption, calculate your own average monthly payment amount.)

Follow those fixed costs with your more variable expenses: food, clothing, healthcare, home maintenance, gifts, and personal care (e.g., haircuts, massage). Transportation costs should also be added here: auto maintenance, gas, parking, bus fare, and so on. As we've already established, those costs often go up and down, sometimes seasonally, sometimes due to medical issues, or sometimes due to a major life change such as a new home or job. But you should still be able to tally what you typically spend in a year for those items and divide by 12 to get a good idea of an average monthly expenditure.

Another item to list should be your expected, or "known," expenses, such as a bill that comes semi-annually, your annual medical deductible, your children's summer camp, your yearly family vacation, or the roof you know you will need to replace in a couple more years.

Next, you will want to make a "payment" to yourself each month. That is the money you are going to use to create and fill each of the following: (1) your household emergency fund, (2) your "Put & Take" account, (3) your daughter's college tuition, and (4) your retirement savings. The best way to determine that monthly payment amount is to start at your anticipated totals for 1 and 2 above, establish a reasonable yet challenging time frame, and work backward, as shown in this example:

- Target: Four years
- Emergency fund will contain $12,000 ($4,000 in monthly expenses for three months)
- Put & Take account will contain $2,500
- Total to put away: $14,500, spread out over 48 months
- $302 monthly payment ($14,500 ÷ 48 mos. = $302)

As your cash flow increases, follow the same process for 3 and 4 above.

Finally, it's time to factor a little fun into your budget—an amount you will let yourself spend each month on life's diversions, such as movies, meals out, tickets, trips, and the like. These are your discretionary funds, and they are the area over which you have the most control. Until you meet your targeted goals and have your emergency fund and Put & Take account fully funded, I recommend that you limit discretionary spending to between one-quarter and one-third of the amount you are putting away each month. Using the case illustrated above, one-quarter to one-third of your $302 monthly payment to yourself is $75 to $100.

Some of you may add up all your expenses and realize your income doesn't come close to covering the amount of money you spend. Time to consider making some adjustments. Others may find that you've added everything up and haven't spent all your income. That's okay—no one says we must spend every dollar we earn!

HERE'S WHAT YOUR BUDGET MIGHT LOOK LIKE SO FAR:

MONTHLY INCOME: *$3,600*

MONTHLY EXPENSES:

Mortgage payment	$1,100
Car payment	$275
College loan	$62
Auto & homeowners insurance	$173
Utilities (electricity, water)	$140
Cable/Internet	$142
Religious affiliation dues	$25
Home maintenance	$100
Clothing/personal care	$110
Medical co-pays	$40
Transportation (gas, parking, bus fare)	$130
Groceries	$600
Known expenses	$180
Self-payment for savings	$302
Discretionary	$175
TOTAL MONTHLY EXPENSES:	$3,554; $46 left for unknowns

MANAGING YOUR BUDGET, OR WHO'S THE BOSS?

And so I have grown up wanting to feel secure when it comes to money, but doing so by treating it as something to be enjoyed, shared, and not given power.

—Alan Cumming, *Not My Father's Son*

You have now taken the most important first steps of developing a budget. Now you need a process to track and monitor it. **It cannot be simply a piece of paper with numbers that you add up and analyze at the end of the year.** You must manage the budget in an ongoing manner. Be sure you have designed a budget that spends less than what you bring in. Look for ways to reduce or eliminate fixed costs as much as possible. After a month or two, look at your actual spending to see how it compares with what you estimated you would spend and then make adjustments as needed. Take note if your bills are going up in any areas, and try to identify the reasons. Again, make any necessary adjustments. Continually look ahead in order to be sure you will have enough to cover everything. Add any new expenses only after you have assessed the impact they will have. Expect the unexpected, and be prepared for it.

You will find that the key to managing your budget is exercising self-control. Resist the temptation to make large purchases—even if you have money left over at the end of several months. Instead, use that surplus to add more flexibility to your budget or to increase the amount you are putting into savings. If you have a shortfall, you may need to consider adjusting your discretionary expenses, such as entertainment and travel, until the shortfall has been corrected.

RECORDKEEPING

Why should we maintain records, hold on to documents, and keep track of our financial commitments? I'll give you several good reasons. First, it is your responsibility to protect yourself by knowing what is owed to you and what your responsibilities and obligations are. In the case of an illness or accident, for example, it is especially critical that you hold on to medical bills that tell you what your insurance company covers and what you need to pay. I hold on to most bills for a year or so, and I keep medical bills for longer periods—in case there is ever a dispute—until the incident is settled.

Second, we need **something in writing to keep us on track.** Many people tend to live in the present; they get caught up in the now and forget decisions they've made in the past—especially the ones that get in the way of what they want to do today. Rationalization is a powerful psychological reality of our minds. According to an article by ChangingMinds.com, "Rationalization is finding 'good reason' for things that we really know are wrong." This article explains in layman's terms one of the core concepts presented in *The Ego and the Mechanisms of Defense* (1936), by Anna Freud, daughter of the iconic scholar and father of psychoanalysis, Sigmund Freud. We want what we want, and we want it now, and we will develop logical support for our decisions/actions. We arrive at the car dealer intending to buy a used car, but then the shiny new models catch our eye, and we end up giving in. We're in the moment, focused on today, and we spend substantially more than we had planned on. If we had visually gone over our budget prior to going to the dealership, we may have been able to stay more focused and catch our rationalization process and avoid making a serious error in judgement.

Third, recordkeeping might help you save money down the road. If interest rates change or better terms become available, you have the information up front to determine if changes make sense. More than once I've helped clients review their loan documents only to find they were paying significantly more than market rate interest. Having documentation of loans, services, and bill paying can protect us from paying too much, like my clients, or from not sufficiently meeting our obligations, which can lead to credit issues and the like. We need to have a record of the terms of our loans, for example, to have an awareness of what is expected of us and what we have promised to do.

I have a client who had a well-written, bumper-to-bumper warranty on a sturdy new van he had purchased. He had forgotten about the warranty coverage when his transmission failed, and he was looking at a $1,800 repair bill. It wasn't until the service manager asked whether he had a warranty package that he remembered paying for one. After hours of searching through boxes of assorted paperwork, he found the warranty—and it was expiring in three days. He lucked out, but lesson learned! Today, he has a well-organized recordkeeping system, including filed warranties and a master list indicating the items covered, the general terms, their financial responsibilities, and the expiration date. He reviews these records twice a year to ensure nothing has changed.

Finally, we keep records because mistakes happen. **Errors are made.** We think we have the bills paid, but one is missing. The department store neglects to credit us for a return and refund. If we need to dispute a bill, we have all our documentation to back up our case. I keep files for at least a year for this purpose.

Store formal documents in a safe place. Design a filing system that works for you so you can easily locate such miscellaneous paperwork as warranty coverage, membership documents, large purchase receipts, etc. Prepare simple outlines of all your loan terms to keep in their files. This makes reviewing your current liabilities easy to do, and you can update and track your pay-off process as you go. Go through your records twice a year to rotate and purge. If you have the technology, scanning the documents can decrease clutter and reduce the space needed to store it all.

The bottom line is that recordkeeping increases your awareness of how and why your financial decisions are interlocked and helps keep you aware of your financial contracts and responsibilities.

This is how you live within your means. This is how you manage your finances in an intelligent and responsible way. It is how you provide for yourself and your family while protecting your assets and preparing for your future. This is spending—and living—with intention!

If money management isn't something you enjoy, consider my perspective. I look at managing my money as if it were a part-time job. The time you spend monitoring your finances will pay off. You can make real money by cutting expenses and earning more interest on savings and investments. I'd challenge you to find a part-time job where you could potentially earn as much money for just an hour or two of your time.

—Laura D. Adams, *Money Girl's Smart Moves to Deal with Your Debt*

CHAPTER 6

MONEY-SAVING TOOLS, TIPS, AND STRATEGIES FROM A FINANCIAL PLANNER

Economics is all about consumption. People either spend money now or they use financial instruments—like bonds, stocks and savings accounts—so they can spend more later.

—Adam Davidson, cohost and founder
of *Planet Money* on NPR

MAKE LISTS!

An idea can only become a reality once it is broken down into organized, actionable elements.

—Scott Belsky, *Making Ideas Happen: Overcoming the Obstacles Between Vision and Reality*

Years ago, I read somewhere that ten minutes of planning will save you an hour in execution. Completing a household project, for example, will go much more smoothly and efficiently if you plan out your steps and the materials you will need in the form of a list. That simple and basic planning concept resonated with me, and since then I've become quite a list maker. Before I go grocery shopping, start my yard work, cook a holiday meal, or launch a new initiative at work, I create a list that will be my road map until the project is completed. I find that when I start with my deadline and work backward, I can allow the time needed for each step and streamline my efforts.

You may be wondering what keeping lists has to do with your money mind-set and managing your finances. I think you will agree that much of what you've read in this book thus far has been about control: controlling your attitude, controlling your spending, and controlling your wants and needs. I believe that when you make lists, you are proactively controlling, or **taking ownership of, your time and efforts**. You are ensuring that whatever task you are about to do, you will be prepared and will not have to disrupt your process. You will minimize the time you spend duplicating efforts, you will eliminate last-minute purchasing by having everything you need at the outset, and you will most certainly keep your stress level at a minimum.

I even take list-making a step further by organizing my grocery list according to the layout of my local supermarket or planning out my day's errands according to where each stop is in relation to my starting and stopping points. By doing that, I seldom forget an item I need to buy. If the hardware store is halfway between the supermarket and the post office, I think of hardware items I know I'll be needing soon so that I won't have to return to the area just a few days later. I have found over and over again that when I prioritize, integrate, and consolidate my lists, I save myself valuable time, not to mention gas!

Here's another idea I think you'll find helpful. If you keep basic lists for a variety of your activities, you can avoid having to reinvent the wheel each time you do that activity. You also will reduce your chances of forgetting important items. Grocery shopping, for example, can start with a basic list that includes many of the staple items you purchase with some frequency. Eggs, milk, bread, and butter can head the list, followed by specific produce, meats, paper goods, and cleaning products. If you're going on a camping trip and pull out your basic camping list, you'll find that the packing process is quicker and more efficient. You'll have your multipurpose flashlight and batteries with you, and you won't have to stop somewhere along the way to buy lesser-quality versions of the items you already have.

And let me leave you with one final thought, particularly concerning larger home maintenance items: Let's say you need a leaf blower and power washer for spring cleaning, and in all likelihood, so do your neighbors. Think of the time and money you all can save by renting those items for a few days and splitting the cost. If you take a few moments to make a list of things that can be shared, then your savings will multiply incrementally. And if your neighbors don't want to rent a leaf blower with you, it may be because they already own one and would be willing to let you borrow it. You'll find that a bottle of wine or plate of homemade scones can go a long way!

> *Being thoughtful includes the willingness to barter, borrow and loan, is being frugal, it is not being cheap.*
>
> **—Nancy J. LaPointe, planner and author**

THE POWER OF A SCHEDULE

Organizing is a journey, not a destination.

—Unknown

The natural partner of list making is scheduling. By planning out your time with purpose and intention, whether it is daily, weekly, monthly, etc., you are remaining in control of another very basic aspect of your life. And, like making a list, creating a schedule will ensure that you meet all your short- and long-term goals, save valuable time and money, and keep your stress factor low. While spontaneity can be fun and teach us flexibility, scheduling our time is part of a proven, responsible approach to achieving what we *need* to in order to accomplish what we *want*.

When you're about to develop a schedule, whether it is for a specific event, a specific time period, or for the completion of a large task, it helps to begin with—you guessed it—a list. For example, in scheduling household activities for spring, start with a list of the things you want to accomplish. Include major priorities (i.e., things that are essential to your life or those that must be done before anything else can be done). Cleaning out and organizing your workshop will allow you to begin some needed repair projects that will require work space. Researching washing machines will prepare you to make a sound and timely purchase the next time there is a sale or before your current machine spins its last cycle. Taking inventory of what's in your garage will help you avoid buying duplicates of tools and recreational items you already own. Finally, amending your garden soil will enable you to put in your vegetable plantings as soon as the weather gets nicer.

Follow your priority activities with other goals that may be less critical. An outdoor concert or weekend away are examples of activities that may be possible *if* you address your priorities first. Consider whether each activity on your list is time sensitive or can be postponed, whether you'll require the assistance or participation of someone else, or whether any external timelines, such as holidays or annual hardware markdowns, will impact your scheduling. Another tip is to build in some down time for yourself. If you think you will finish the workshop on Saturday, perhaps Sunday would be a nice opportunity to relax, reflect, and catch up on your reading, rather than tackling another large project. Lastly, give yourself plenty of lead time, and be prepared for the unavoidable delays that happen in life, whether they are due to illness, mechanical issues, weather, or other people's actions. As you well know, life happens while we're busy making other plans.

Scheduling your time allows you to live a life of intention while not missing out on opportunities that may never present themselves again. Scheduling your goals for the present, and seeing how scheduling works in your favor, lets you remain focused on and committed to your goals for the future. I promise you, the long-term payoffs will be extremely rewarding!

DON'T NICKEL AND DIME YOUR DREAMS AWAY

There is a difference between dreaming and doing.
—Anonymous

You know the feeling. You go online to check your account balance, expecting to see a number that fits into an approximate range you have in mind. But when you see the actual number, you're taken aback. You think it must be a mistake. You don't recall spending so much money. *Where did all the money go?* you ask yourself, frantically. You know you've made no major purchases or big withdrawals in the last month, so you take a closer look to figure out how you could have blown through half your paycheck without even being aware of it.

Suddenly, it hits you. Those modest lunches, refreshing lattes, and quick trips to the drugstore have cost you nearly $500 in the past month! Then there were the birthday gifts you needed to buy, the candy purchase to support a fundraiser, a handful of books at the bookstore, and a couple of parking lot payments that added another $170. And that's not all. Now you remember that a few weeks earlier, you gave your neighbor $30 to mow your lawn, saw a movie with a friend, had some extra keys made, paid a few highway tolls, bought some bottles of water at the park, and took advantage of a grocer's special and filled your freezer with ground beef. Aha! You're beginning to see the light.

If your goal is to have your house paid off by age 50, then let's assume you need to save $600 per month and get an average return of 6 percent over the next 15 years. If all goes as planned, you will have the lump sum to have the house paid off as you dreamt by age 50. This is the action needed to accomplish your dream. Now, how are you going to do this? **Your net income has not increased by $600 per month simply because you now have an action step.** You and yours need to look at your budget and determine how you are going to make $600 available for your dream.

Reducing spending by $600 per month, if you have not been saving $600 or more before is daunting. Break it down to weekly, then daily amounts. The $600 becomes $133.33 per week (4.35 weeks in a month) and 19.04 per day. This breakdown makes it more palatable; in bite-size pieces it becomes an achievable goal. You may realize you can save $45 per week, just by taking your lunch to work three times a week. Save $20 drinking your own coffee instead of the latte at the coffee shop. Now you're down to $68.33 a week or $9.76 per day. So you still go out with your buddies for lunch twice a week, but now you order the special, saving $10 per week. You only have two beers on Friday without eating appetizers, saving $22 per week. You now have $36.33 a week to still save or $163.48 for the month. Now you look at the weekends and eliminate eating Sunday breakfast out and going to events every weekend. Now you do one or the other every other weekend. Bravo, you now have made $600 available to your dream. Prior to these steps, you were spending a nickel here, a dime there, and your dreams were not on track to become reality.

The fact is that most of us do not realize how quickly all these minor purchases add up. It feels to us as though we've just been living our day-to-day lives, when in reality, we've been nickel-and-diming our dreams away.

Whether your dream is to own your own home, send your children to college, buy a small business, or retire at age 62, you have a vision that represents your personal goals. Your goals hold particular meaning for you, as they are indeed yours and no one else's, and they embody your authentic views and expectations of yourself. So you must ask yourself if your daily latte is more important than your life's visions or if giving up lunches out with colleagues would be worth it to achieve your dream. You always have the option of putting off those sacrifices, but for every year you delay it, you are adding a year onto your waiting time.

For many people, the vision of someday owning a home or retiring at age 62 may, frankly, be too far in the future to inspire their new money mind-set. If you're one of those people, start by bringing your goal into the more immediate future and making it more accessible, so it has a greater impact. Now ask yourself if you'd rather have lunch and a latte or be able to escape to the ocean over the weekend. I think you already know the answer.

Here's another tip: In the same way that serious dieters lose more weight if they write down everything they eat, you can learn to keep close track of what you are spending by writing down all your monthly purchases, large and small. Had you kept an updated list of the lattes, lunches, keys, parking fees, tolls, and gifts listed above, you would have seen how quickly those numbers were adding up, and you would have avoided the shock of discovering a low bank balance.

Finding ways to pare down your miscellaneous spending will seem daunting at first. Over time, however, as you learn to limit nickel-and-dime spending to true necessities and realize you still have plenty of quality of life, it will become easier. You will feel more focused and in control. This will be your new habit, your new mind-set, and believe me, it will reward you!

SALES AND CREDIT CARDS—THE EVIL TWINS

Slight was the thing I bought,
Small was the debt I thought,
Poor was the loan at best—
God! but the interest!

—Paul Laurence Dunbar, African-American
poet, novelist, and playwright

Over the years, my mother has offered me many words of wisdom. Some I've been more open to receiving than others, of course. But one of her truest pieces of advice, with which I couldn't agree more, is, "A sale does not benefit you unless you were going to buy it anyway." Take a moment to think about that. The local department store has a sale on jeans, shoes, or rice cookers, and it is an amazing price reduction. Your supermarket is running a great special on milk and eggs. You want to take advantage of these sales. A voice in your head says you would be foolish not to. Look at all the money you'd "save." Another voice argues that you have all the jeans and shoes you really need, all the milk and eggs you have room for in your refrigerator, and you seldom cook rice.

Despite all the rationalization against checking out the sale, most people—believe it or not—would listen to the first voice, the path of least resistance, and go shopping. If you know you're one of them, I encourage you to think about your choice next time and stay home instead. If you *need* jeans or shoes, okay, different story. *But chances are you don't, so why fall prey to the department stores' promotions?* When you make a purchase and put it on a credit card, you will have to pay them back—with interest. But aren't you smarter than that? *You* can outsmart *them*, you know. Don't even bring sales flyers in the door. Drop them in the recycle bin before you come in the house. Only search through promotional ads that are related to a current, specific shopping objective you have. Then, decide on your price range and your spending limit before setting foot in a store. Bottom line:

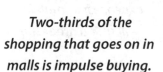

Two-thirds of the shopping that goes on in malls is impulse buying.

—Paco Underhill, author of *Why We Buy: The Science of Shopping*

Actually two-thirds of the entire economy is impulse buying.

—Doug McPherson, author of *The Psychology of Impulse Buying*

Make sure that your purchase is based on intent and need and is not a reaction to a sales promotion.

Impulse spending on sales does not just occur in department stores or for clothing. Grocery stores and flyers are also set up to encourage buying based on the store's objectives. Hardware stores and household goods shops such as Target or Shopko are also vying for your dollars and for getting you to act on their timeline. Stores are designed to visually attract you to act spontaneously. **Have a defined reason, supported by a list, when you go to the stores.** Go to meet your objective and remain within your allotment. Using cash in your pocket or your debit card is still spending, still depleting your resources. I encourage you not to browse or shop around but to go in with your intentions and leave with what you came to buy in the first place.

Beware of little expenses; a small leak will sink a great ship.

—Benjamin Franklin

And then there are credit cards, those magical plastic devices that bring families together, send them all to Disneyland, and promise to make everyone's dreams come true. But the reality behind all the happy smiles is that you are using someone else's money to make a purchase, and the debt that follows as a result is a high price to pay. For some, it is a treacherous trap out of which they may never escape. Emotionally, and in turn physically, individuals and families are negatively affected by their debt load. I frequently hear from my clients that they feel ashamed, sick, and frustrated—all related to their credit card debt. I tell them to imagine burning actual cash when paying interest on credit cards. They tell me it works!

Let's play out a typical credit card scenario: You wander into a stylish boutique (despite having no available funds with which to shop), and you fall in love with all the fabulous fashions you see. Plus, everything is "on sale." You can't resist the temptation, and the next thing you know, you've made a total purchase of $300. You head home, excited to wear your new clothes. Two weeks later, the credit card bill comes. The balance is $300, but you really only *have* to pay the $15 minimum. So you write a check for the minimum. Next month, you owe $278.84, you pay the minimum $15 dollars. At this time you paid $30.00 in

> *A credit card should be a source of convenience for you, not a revenue source for the credit card company.*
>
> **—Nancy J. LaPointe, planner and author**

payments. Please note $278.84 is the debt listed on the second bill, you made two payments of $30.00, $278.84 plus $30.00 =$308.84. A year from now, if you continue paying the minimum, you will owe $163.06. In 1 year and 11 months you will have the credit card debt paid off and would have $59.36 in interest. How many times did your wear these clothes? You may have never realized it before, but this kind of exploitation can go on for months or years.

And did you only use this credit card for this purchase? If new purchases are tacked on, a multiple effect continues. If you, over a period of a year, put $300 each month on your credit card, you will have charged a total $3,600.00, and your total debt with be

$4,170, your minimum payment will now be $166.80. If you add nothing else to your balance and continue sending in minimum payments, it will take you 10 years and 6 months to pay off your $4,170 credit card debt and $2,375.57 of this amount will be interest payments. You paid $2,375.57 to borrow $3,600.

You don't have to play at that game. Rather than thinking of a credit card as a great way to buy things even when you have no money, think of it instead just as a tool of convenience when you need an easy way to make a secure payment. Use it only when you know you have the cash to back up your purchase and can pay your credit card bill in full within one month.

Then, memorize my Ten Commandments of Avoiding Credit Card Debt:

NANCY'S TEN COMMANDMENTS OF AVOIDING CREDIT CARD DEBT

A credit card allows you to transcend time, for it allows you to put off until tomorrow what you bought today, while you are still paying for what you bought yesterday.

—Robert Morrissette, Canadian writer

1. Thou shall not use credit cards without thoughtful intention and a plan to cover the expense.

2. Thou shall not carry credit card balances forward from month to month.

3. Thou shall not purchase everyday items thou cannot pay for with cash, a check, or a debit card.

4. Thou shall not go on vacations and pay for them afterward.

5. Thou shall not put thyself in harm's way at local malls, pricey bistros, and outdoor art shows.

6. Thou shall vow to never again pay retail but instead, find less expensive ways to buy the identical items.

7. Thou shall learn to say no to thyself.

8. Thou shall not act on every sales promotion or credit card offering.

9. Thou shall never borrow money for any reason that is not a necessity or emergency.

10. Thou shall be mindful, intentional, and responsible when it comes to managing thy finances!

Credit card interest payments are the dumbest money of all.

—Hill Harbor, author, *Conversation with a Brother*

FIFTY PAINLESS WAYS TO TRIM COSTS

Watch your finances like a hawk.

—H. Jackson Brown, Jr., author, *Life's Little Instruction Book*

As a financial planner, I am committed to finding ways my clients can live for less and save money, so they can maximize what they have and achieve their dreams for the future. It doesn't stop there; I practice what I preach. Through the years, I've accumulated a lengthy list of helpful tips for trimming expenses associated with both necessities and non-necessities that allow us to run our homes, feed our families, do a little traveling, and live full, healthy, meaningful lives. On the following pages I am happy to share some of these tips with you.

Reducing cost related to necessities is about being wiser and more thoughtful regarding how you spend. Use less, be more efficient in your use, and you will see the difference!

1. Restrict your use of credit and loans; pay cash whenever you possibly can, especially for vehicles.

2. Look for the lowest possible lending rate when taking out a mortgage or car loan.

3. Borrow money only for necessities.

4. Pay your bills on time, and you will never incur late fees.

5. Why buy a brand new automobile when a good, reliable used car can save you thousands?

6. If you put money away every month, you'll be able to buy your next car with cash and avoid paying interest on a loan.

7. Never sign an auto leasing agreement without getting an impartial "second opinion." Leasing agreements are seldom designed to benefit the consumer.

8. When purchasing a home, remember the smaller the home, the less it costs to heat and maintain.

9. Buying a one-story home will enable you to complete many maintenance tasks yourself and avoid paying others for their services.

10. See if your utilities providers will come and do a free assessment of your home to maximize your energy or water efficiency.

11. Seal and/or replace older doors and windows.

12. Cable companies come out with new plans all the time; you may be able to get more for less by signing up for a new package.

13. Get a cell phone plan based on your actual use; don't pay for services you don't really use.

14. Find affordable packages by taking advantage of competition between cell phone carriers. (Same with Internet carriers.)

15. Plan meals ahead of time and take your week's meal plan and a shopping list to the supermarket with you.

16. Do not shop when you are hungry, anxious, or depressed.

17. Prepare dinners that tomorrow can double as a lunch.

18. It takes the same amount of time if you cook in larger quantities and freeze half of what you cook.

19. Invest in a small vacuum packer to keep your food items fresher for a longer period of time.

20. Use coupons only if an item was on your list anyway; don't buy it just because you found a coupon.

21. Find a storage space near your kitchen where you can keep items you bought in quantity at a greatly reduced price. Keep track of your inventory.

22. Get into the habit of shopping in bulk sections whenever possible for grains, nuts, seeds, and dried fruits.

23. Stop paying for bottled water. Bring your own thermos wherever you go. (When eating out, forget expensive beverages, and order tap water.)

24. Many insurance premiums will vary depending on how many payments you make per year. Annually and semi-annually are less expensive.

25. Research auto insurance providers every three to five years to ensure that you're still getting the best value.

26. Bundling auto, homeowners, and/or life insurance can usually save you money.

27. Seek health providers who offer wellness packages or reduce fees if you pay in cash.

28. Don't be afraid of using generic pharmaceuticals, including both prescription and over-the-counter products.

29. Look for mail-order and online prescription services that offer lower prices for the same medications.

30. If you eat well, exercise, get enough rest, and follow your doctor's recommendations, you will be rewarded not only with better health but also with far fewer medical bills.

31. Often, when doctors know you are struggling to pay your bills, they will be willing to negotiate a flat fee to

satisfy your bill; have an honest conversation with your provider, and share your financial concerns.

32. Consider paying a lower tuition at a community college for your child's first year or two and then transfer if desired.

33. Seek employers who provide or assist with education tuition.

34. Graduating from a four-year academic program doesn't have to happen in four years; stretching it out allows you to work part-time and pay tuition as you can, rather than taking out a student loan you will be saddled with for many years to come.

35. Cohabitate and share transportations costs while a student.

36. Buy used books whenever possible, and look in the library for short-term reading assignments.

37. Entertainment on campus is typically less expensive than elsewhere, plus you avoid parking and transportation costs.

38. Take advantage of student discounts for shopping, entertainment, healthcare, etc.

39. Seek employment on or near campus to greatly reduce transportation costs and maximize your time.

40. Research opportunities for resident advisors; you may get free or reduced room and board.

41. Do not shop as entertainment or a social event; treat it as work and get the job done.

42. Find the discount clothing stores in your community and stop paying full retail prices in department stores.

43. Consignment shops are a low-cost resource for expensive clothing that may have been worn only once or twice—or not at all.

44. Shop off-season.

45. Keeping your weight constant allows you to build a wardrobe over time and still fit into it several years from now.

46. Items of clothing that can be worn with several things are your best buy.

47. If feasible, shopping in a different state can save you in sales taxes, but calculate whether you will still be saving after spending more on gas to get there.

48. Try getting haircuts every six or seven weeks rather than once a month, and do a little trimming between appointments.

49. Look into purchasing a home haircutting tool; it will usually pay for itself the first time you use it.

50. Forsake costly concert and theater tickets in favor of free and low-cost community happenings, such as outdoor music festivals, athletic events, cultural presentations, and local nonprofit fundraisers.

CHAPTER 7

LOOKING TO THE FUTURE

One of the greatest gifts you can give your kids is to prepare
them to be responsible, empowered adults around money.

—Unknown

TEACHING YOUR CHILDREN ABOUT MONEY

A family is an organization, a one-of-a-kind structure that is very basic to our society. Within the family, the parents are the leaders, the chief co-officers. They serve important roles, and they need to be recognized. They shape and determine the family's focus and culture. They make the all-important decisions concerning education, activities, church and community involvement, what values will be taught, and what behaviors are and are not acceptable. I have observed that too often in families there is no central focus and no prioritization of goals and values.

Parents whose own parents were good money teachers felt more knowledgeable about managing their personal finances and investing matters than those whose parents did not prepare them well.

Among the former group, 73% and 44% said they were knowledgeable about personal finances and investing, respectively, compared with 59% and 21% for the latter group.[15]

90% of young people say that it is important to learn about managing money.[16]

The parents' roles are to support and develop family members as individuals and as members of the family. It is work, and like the traditional recognized work, each member has a role or two. Unlike traditional work, however, success is not defined, and emotions cannot be suppressed but need to be considered as part of the decision-making process.

I see two major chief officer roles within the family "corporation"—the financial officer and the operations officer. In traditional work, these roles are clearly differentiated, but in families, not so much. With family responsibilities and roles, there is always going to be some overlap subject to circumstances driven by the nature of the work. Having a series of conversations, acknowledging the need to define the family's priorities and then the steps needed to support those, can be powerful.

Let's look at a very basic operational activity, such as the feeding of the family. What is the decision-making process around meal planning? Is a weekly meal plan used? Are costs monitored, or is money just spent with little or no consideration to the expense? Do vacations and ball games dominate the family focus with little attention given to daily expenses such as groceries?

---

15 T. Rowe Price Survey, 2014
16 RBS Group MoneySense Research Panel, 2011 Report

Reality for most families is that all are important. The questions parents need to keep in mind are (1) whether they have sufficiently reflected on and prioritized their values in order to live with intention; and (2) how they can include their children in the process so everyone's on the same page with regard to what's important to them as a family and what their goals are. What are our top-three objectives, and do they complement each other? Are they obtainable, and at what price? Integrating activities, financial and operational, for the family's determined mission and objectives is the role of the parents. It is not a static, written-in-stone mission statement but a dynamic and evolving framework without which random activities, disconnect, and potential for stress and frustration increase tremendously. If the parents are not partners, with shared values and supportive activities, the family may end up dysfunctional beyond the norm.

What do you remember about your childhood in regard to money? Many of us heard often, *"Money doesn't grow on trees."* Seems a silly analogy, but think about it. Leaves just happen. They renew consistently. Some fall off once a year, but the next spring they're back. Most trees are not cultivated or maintained but are enjoyed freely.

When global investment management firm T. Rowe Price conducted their 2014 "Parents, Kids & Money" survey, one-third of the parents surveyed reported that they avoid having conversations with their children about money. Three-quarters said they had some reluctance to talk with their kids about financial topics, most often because they don't want their kids to worry about finances.

On the other hand, money and income do not just happen. One cultivates it by the sweat of their brow, their skills, their creativity, and by intention. **Children need to have an understanding of that basic connection between money and work.** This can happen by openly discussing the work of the parent and of friends and relatives and by allowing a child to see and participate in that work. Strive to let them see the rewards of a job well done, a sense of accomplishment or contribution. Share with them your recognition of other peoples' skills and contributions, such as those of a nurse, a mechanic, a teacher, or a computer programmer.

Don't wait until your children are older to start talking about money. Start early! Let them see what money looks like. Many children learn to count using coins. Later on, talk in the presence of your children as you decide on things you're going to buy for the family. Gift-giving provides some great lessons about spending money. When your child is invited to a birthday party, for example, talk about the process of buying gifts. Encourage your child to ask his friend what he would like as a gift. Or offer creative alternatives to gifts that cost money, such as gifts of activities (sleepovers, fishing outings, day hikes on the beach) or items that are crafted by the family.

Lead by example. If children see their parents buying at will for themselves, they're being taught that money is available freely. Practice restraint so they can see that these limitations are shared by everyone in the family. Keep in mind that children need a sense of security, so there is nothing to be gained by emphasizing the sometimes-critical ups and downs of family money. Assure your children that you have enough for the things the family needs and that they are not to worry about whether the family is going to "run out" of money.

Young children especially don't always understand the concepts of not having enough money or where the money comes from. I once spent an afternoon with a friend and her spirited six-year-old, who pleaded with her mother to buy her a new toy. "We don't have enough money to buy that toy today," said my friend, to which her daughter replied, helpfully, "Then let's just go to the bank machine and get some more!" To the child, the ATM was where their money came from. After all, she had watched many times, as both her parents had withdrawn cash and put it in their wallets. Once again, children should learn that money comes from our jobs and from working hard. We get a certain amount every week/month to buy our food and the other things we *need*, and we don't always have enough to buy the things we *want*. And there is a difference.

Families need to acknowledge their financial abilities and limitations. When children want to know why one family has things in their home that other families do not or why one family gets to go on a great vacation while other families do not, you can explain it to them. I remember my parents explaining that we did not have quite as much money as another family we knew and that we were using our money to go visit our grandparents rather than buy another TV like the other family. Also, we had four kids, and they only had two, so we had more mouths to feed and had to spend more of our money on food. And it was made abundantly clear to us that money was not freely available; **it was earned through work and effort.**

Don't be afraid to share your family's financial capabilities and priorities with your children. Have the strength to say no when you need to. Be consistent about it. You don't need to go into income inequities each time you say no. But you can be proactive and intentional, explaining that a new TV/boat/dog/bike is not a family priority right now. Perhaps you're saving for something else they will enjoy or benefit from. In that case, share that with them. The worst thing that can happen is that your children will experience delayed gratification, consequences, and self-discipline.

Another concept children can learn is the illogical incongruity between the amount one earns and the importance of the work they do, as well as how hard they have to work to get their jobs done. I encourage you to present this in a nonjudgmental manner. Point out that as individuals we each have passions—whether they be teaching, healing, building, or maintaining roads—and that while each person's passion can become a contribution to our community, compensation does not always match the difficulty or importance of the work. But also emphasize that there is personal happiness in working in a field you have a passion and skill for and that money isn't the only kind of reward.

MONEY AND YOUR TEENAGER

Only one in five parents (20 percent) involve their teen in family budgeting and spending decisions to a great extent, so they can learn by doing.

—Schwab Parents & Money Survey, 2008

When we were old enough to make decisions about spending our own money, my siblings and I often learned lessons the hard way (I once had to wear the same two pairs of jeans to school every day for a year), but we did learn them. As we got older, the volume grew and the variety expanded of the things we wanted. I began to look for babysitting jobs to afford the riding boots and horse blanket I wanted. Those babysitting jobs were my first lessons in the disconnect between hard work and the size of a paycheck.

Remember that teenagers are wired to learn from direct experience. Picture this: It's Wednesday night and, as the parents, you are planning your weekend entertainment. You have budgeted a certain amount for the month. In front of your teenage child, go over your options—the base costs as well as anticipated related expenses. Discuss the values and benefits of each option, especially as they relate to what is important to you, and make a choice. Let your kids hear that when making choices, there are several things to consider beyond costs, such as the value of the time we're going to spend, the opportunities we will have to interact with others, the lessons we can learn, and so on. **Give them opportunities to participate**, and encourage this type of reflection as part of the process.

Junior Achievement and the Allstate Foundation released their 2014 Teens and Personal Finance survey in which 56 percent of teenagers predicted they will be as financially well-off or better than their parents—a 37 percent drop from 2011's 89 percent.

When it comes to participation in things like school activities and sports teams, provide your teenager with a budget so she can learn to balance her options with affordability. Remind her that affordability is not only measured in dollars but also in time, sleep, impact on grades, and the ability to put forth the effort required. If dancing lessons or cheerleading are going to create a financial strain for the family, you may need to revisit your budget and make adjustments, and you can share that information with your teen. Kids need to see that something we want or need today may mean we have to go without something else tomorrow. Maybe only one camping weekend this year instead of two. Maybe less money to spend on summer clothes. These are life skills, and you are doing your job as a parent when you give your kids opportunities to learn them.

HANDS-ON MONEY LESSONS

The most valuable lesson you can teach your kids about money is that it needs to be earned. It is a *two-way process*. You make or give or do something, and you get something back, in this case, money. It is not an entitlement. Parents work hard for the money they have, and as the grown-ups in the house, they get to decide how the money is to be spent.

Kids, too, should have ways to earn money. **Funds earned by children are truly the first building blocks toward their financial future.** It is a great opportunity for parents and other significant people in a child's life to make a lifelong impact in an area that is so fundamental.

Thoughts differ widely regarding giving kids allowance (paying them) when they simply participate in the family or fulfill their basic obligations. I've seen kids clean up their own bedrooms and then go get money from their parents just for doing it. Basic activities like setting or clearing the table become part of a list of household chores that, if all are completed in a timely fashion, are rewarded with a weekly allowance.

I tend to lean the other way. I think setting the table and keeping our rooms clean are basic responsibilities that everyone in a family has, and as such, they don't warrant a monetary reward. If the chores and the reward are seen as a package deal, a youngster might feel there is a choice involved. "I'd rather not have my allowance if it means I have to clean my room," I once heard a 12-year-old boy say. But picking up his clothes and participating in family life shouldn't be a choice. I feel it's actually one of a kid's main jobs right now, and frankly, it's the dues he pays for the roof over his head! Instead, look for earning activities that are measurable. Make them matters of convenience for the parents as opposed to core contributions to the functioning of the home and family.

> Parents when asked to identify the topics they wish they had learned more about when they were teenagers, the greatest percentage (57 percent) choose "money management."[17]

RETIREMENT: A JOURNEY TO PREPARE FOR

You can be young without money, but you can't be old without it.

—Tennessee Williams, playwright

I admit it's a huge jump to go from giving kids an allowance to thinking about retirement. But for people who are hovering close to the latter, I'm told the whole thing just seems like a quick flash in time anyway. "Seems like just yesterday my son was born," a friend said to me recently. Now he's about to become a grandfather. *How did THAT happen?*

Ah, retirement! Just the word conjures visions of card games and gardening, poolside leisure, and extended trips to exotic destinations. It's the well-earned reward for all the days we had to awaken before the rooster, for all the soccer games we had to miss,

---

17 Kenton Research Parent and Money research, 2008

for all the nights we ate cold dinners alone long after the rest of the family had eaten theirs. In retirement, we're our own bosses. Every day can be Saturday, and there's no place we have to be. The rigid routines we once had to follow are but a thing of the past. Good riddance!

Or maybe not. The truth is that, for many, retirement looks very little like the delightful picture we just envisioned. Life is every bit the struggle it once was, except now there is no income. Millions of people find themselves in that position today. BusinessInsider.com reported in 2014 that Americans have spent more time planning their vacations than their retirement. I bet if they had it to do over again, they'd do things differently.

> Almost half of adults were not actively thinking about financial planning for retirement, with 24 percent saying they had given only a little thought to financial planning for their retirement and another 25 percent saying they had done no planning at all. Of those who have given at least some thought to retirement planning and plan to retire at some point, 25 percent didn't know how they will pay their expenses in retirement.[18]

If you are still in your working years, **how much time are *you* investing in your own vision?** Are you positioning yourself to enjoy a relaxing, secure, worry-free retirement? Are you planning with intention, giving your values and priorities full attention in designing your life?

---

18 *Report on the Economic Well-Being of U.S. Households,* Federal Reserve, 2013

It is easy to understand why some people avoid it. Those leisure hours are only part of the picture. The other parts have to do with health problems, mobility issues, the loss of so many loved ones, and our own eventual demise. It's reality, and it's no one's favorite subject. I think many folks are afraid that the minute they start planning for their retirement, their knees will give out, their hair will turn gray, and their hearing will go. No one I know is in any hurry to be *there.*

Like so many other things, it's about attitude. Yes, your knees probably will give out, but how you cope with it and prepare for it is the real issue. Millions of retirees are having the time of their lives, making the most of what they have, and appreciating it more often and more deeply than they ever did before. They do not see retirement as the end of the journey. For them, it's simply a new and different phase of their lives, a new adventure to squeeze into the span of their lifetimes. And all the lessons they've learned and the wisdom they've gained now give them the confidence to enjoy their lives to the fullest. *If they've done the planning, that is.*

Just as we start dreaming of retirement right after college, so we can start preparing for that journey early or just before embarking. The sooner we start preparing, the more likely we are to be ready for it and to have considered all possibilities. The retirement cornerstone may be financial freedom, but as we know, finances are not all there is to life. Relationships with friends and family, involvement in activities from golf, gardening, nonprofit volunteering, exercise, to writing your memoirs are all tied in to having the retirement of your dreams. The work on those aspects of your life can start prior to actual retirement.

 One in three couples disagree as to their ideal vision for retirement. While men are significantly more likely to envision indulging in their favorite sports, women are more likely to envision spending time with family, enjoying hobbies and volunteering in their local community.[19]

Approximately four in ten couples (38 percent) who aren't yet retired disagree as to the lifestyle they expect to live in retirement.[20]

As for the business side of things, start by taking an inventory of your present resources. Know what you are earning on your investments, pension opportunities, and Social Security. Understand the structure of your debt and your home layout. Acknowledge inflation rate and sequence of returns on investments, discretionary or flexible expenses, taxes, as well as health changes and essential needs. Actively pursue the development of skills and relationships that will support the life you want in retirement. **Think of it as a journey into a new phase of life. And like any journey, do not go unprepared.**

The percentage of retirees indicating they are very confident about paying for basic expenses has stayed level at 33 percent (statistically equivalent to the 34 percent observed in 2009).[21]

WORKING WITH A FINANCIAL PLANNER

A good financial plan is a road map that shows us exactly how the choices we make today will affect our future.

—Alexa Von Tobel, author of *Financially Fearless*

19 2013 Fidelity Investments Couples Retirement Study
20 2013 Fidelity Investments Couples Retirement Study
21 Retirement Confidence Survey, 2012

I couldn't end this book without taking a few moments to educate my readers on the benefits of working with CERTIFIED FINANCIAL PLANNER™ practitioners. It may seem like shameless self-promotion, but I assure you it is the one remaining piece of the puzzle that we've been talking about on these pages.

I am a Certified Financial Planning Practitioner (CFP®). I can help you work on the foundations of your financial security and support you in living the life you have always wanted for yourself. I am the first to admit that I cannot fill a cavity, build a house, set a broken arm, or design an expansion bridge. If you needed those things to be done, you would *not* want me to be the one to do them. And you wouldn't attempt them yourself, either. You would go instead to the professionals who have been highly trained to do those jobs, and there, you'd be in good, competent hands and you would end up with what you went there for.

Fondulas research found that those who work with CFP® professionals—financial planners who have met rigorous competency standards and who have agreed to comply with strict ethical standards—had higher levels of satisfaction, were more likely to say they received a plan with realistic financial goals, and were more likely to feel their financial needs and objectives were addressed.[22]

So I hope you will give equal consideration to letting an educated, experienced professional assist you with planning for your financial future, which is no less important than those other jobs which you would never dream of tackling.

Here are some things to know: First, financial planning, at its core, is cash flow management. If you're living in today's world, you are dealing with cash flow. The foundation of any financial

---

22 Fondulas consumer survey, 2012

plan is one's current financial situation with regard to income and expenses (i.e., cash flow). Just as important are having the motivation and capacity to strengthen or modify one's current and future circumstances.

Financial planning is a process of determining and developing a plan or program to support your life goals financially. It can be relatively simple or quite complex, depending on your resources, objectives, and values. The process, as practiced by a CERTIFIED FINANCIAL PLANNER™ practitioner, is defined on the CFP® website. It can be focused on a specific topic, such as retirement planning or investments, fully comprehensive, or it can be a combination of a few topics. You will see on the website the basic topics are (1) current financial situation, (2) protection planning, (3) investment planning, (4) tax planning, (5) retirement planning, and (6) estate planning. Tied in with those are major purchases, family development, education, and business-related matters.

You start by determining your commitment to developing a comprehensive strategy that will align your financial activities with your values and actions. You may have just left home, been married ten years, or be retiring in five. If you're like many people, you have a financial plan in place by default but not by intention. Building a plan by intention takes a willingness to reflect and take ownership of decisions and actions, along with a willingness to change or adjust behavior. If you're willing to change your course, to change your actions and behavior, and to address your short- and long-term objectives, you're ready to start the planning process.

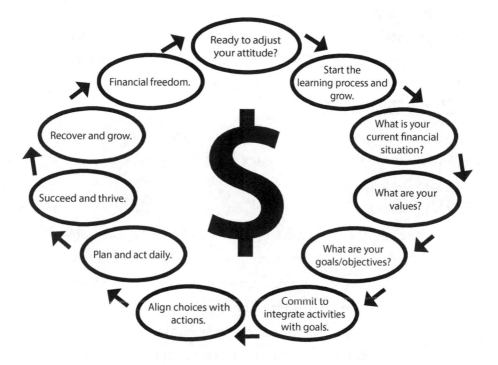

Once you have made the decision to develop an intentional plan, we begin by dissecting your present financial plan. We analyze your current situation, review your income and spending, and estimate your financial commitments. This is often the first time you will have compiled all the expenses of living in your home. This can be an eye opener.

As the process unfolds, you and your planner will define and prioritize your values and objectives. Working together, you will explore options and the affordability and consequences of those options. You also will integrate your cash resources to your goals and objectives in a manner that is sustainable and with a plan you can commit to. The plan will address the possible and the probable and include provisions for life's curveballs.

In a nutshell, you get started with financial planning by being mentally and emotionally ready. That is when you contact a qualified professional, a *Certified Financial Planning practitioner*.

SEEKING GOOD ADVICE

Money is the opposite of the weather. Nobody talks about it, but everybody does something about it.

—Rebecca Johnson

I'm often asked what to look for and how to make sure you're getting good advice when selecting a professional to assist you with your finances. There are conflicting interpretations of what true financial planning is. Today, "financial planning" is a generic term used for anything from rudimentary budgeting to complex business transitions and estate planning. It can describe an analysis of investments, be a tool for promoting product sales, or be a method for cohesively integrating a family's legacy in a manner that is sustainable. The College of Financial Planning, the Certified Financial Planning Board (CFP®), and the many members of the Financial Planning Association (FPA) are striving to reinforce and develop the professionalism of Certified Financial Planning practitioners. They are educating the public with a standard definition of financial planning and the elements of a financial plan. (If you're interested in researching their standards and code of ethics, I invite you to visit the CFP® website [www.*cfp.net*] and the FPA website [www.*onefpa.org*].)

Establishing financial planning as a well-defined, certifiable profession has been a lengthy process, not unlike those that CPAs, MDs, and attorneys at law have struggled with. At one time, state regulators and society-at-large allowed individuals to promote themselves as doctors, dentists, or attorneys, despite their having little or no formal training. If you felt you were qualified, you were in business! Doctors bonded together to eliminate from their ranks and protect the public from those who were not qualified to practice medicine, and now, thankfully, those days have passed. Today, there is a level of uniformly accepted standards for education, experience, and training, along with ongoing reviews and continuing education for those professions. Nationally, we do not have a uniform standard for a practitioner of financial planning. The federal and state governments manage a series of tests and regulations for advising clients on investments. But investments are only one element of financial planning, as defined by the CFP® Board.

The CFP® Board requirements for certification, education, adherence to ethics, and continuing education are what we have in place presently as a national standard for Certified Financial Planning practitioners. **To my knowledge, it is not required in any state to practice.** Like doctors and attorneys in the past, if you feel you have the knowledge, you can put up your shingle. Your resident state, or the state you're practicing in, along with the federal government's Securities and Exchange-related agencies, may or may not be concerned with your business practices, depending on your activities. Selling marketable securities is heavily regulated, as it should be.

The research shows that 82 percent of consumers believe that a financial planner is the same as a "financial advisor;" 70 percent believe a financial planner is the same as a "wealth manager;"

and 68 percent believe a financial planner is the same as an "investment advisor."[23]

If you're looking to get your taxes done by someone other than yourself, you know you have three choices: a tax preparer, an accountant, or a CPA. Each one has a different level of training, education, and responsibility to you as a client. These standards and definitions developed over time, and the general public knows the difference between a storefront tax preparer and a CPA. A prudent individual seldom confuses the expertise of a nurse with that of a doctor or a paralegal with an attorney. Likewise, what has confused the public has been that home and auto insurance agents are now offering financial planning services to their clients, and investment brokers who pass an exam provide comprehensive financial plans, for an extra fee, of course. How can you know who is and is not qualified to offer planning and from whom you will be getting the best kind of advice?

Data from Cerulli Associates, a leading industry research firm, reveal that in 2013, over 166,000 financial advisors self-identified as members of a financial planning focused practice.

Remember: You want an active, CERTIFIED FINANCIAL PLANNER™ practitioner who is fee-based or fee-only. If your practitioner is fee-based, have an understanding and be comfortable with their platform and broker dealer requirements for offering tools and products. A larger range of options and a lack of quotas are preferred. I recommend reviewing the individual's employment history and background of possible disciplinary actions. If

---

23 The Financial Planning Coalition White Paper, released October 24th, 2014

it's not offered to you, ask to see it. Be comfortable with his or her overall level of experience and, specifically, with any areas you are particularly concerned about in regard to your own financial goals. (Visit http://brokercheck.finra.org/Search/Search to review the record of your current or prospective planner/advisor.)

The two websites mentioned above are where you can start. They are to financial planners what the American Medical Association is to doctors. They are striving to set up barriers to entry, educational requirements, and binding practice standards so the public can be confident in the qualifications of certified practitioners. They are motivated by their values and ethics to clarify and define financial planning.

> Cerulli then verified the practice type by analyzing additional data and determined that only 38 percent of the self-identified financial planners actually had financial planning focused practices. In other words, over 100,000 financial advisors incorrectly self-identified as being part of a financial planning practice.[24]

I also recommend seeking referrals from people you respect and trust. Remember, though, that everyone gives advice based on their own filters, values, and personal code of ethics. Interview several qualified candidates. If they are not participating actively in the planning process, two or more active plans monthly, I would be concerned. Complete your due diligence, and then trust your instincts.

Remember, if you're seeking professional assistance and advice, these are the professionals. We go to professionals for their

---

24 Cerulli 2013 Advisor Metrics Report

knowledge and analysis of matters we cannot do on our own. You hire them for a reason, so expect to have to take actions you did not conceive of on your own or that you may have dismissed as not relevant. Never go to any professional with blind faith. Ask questions, learn, be observant, and have an understanding of the rationale behind the advice you are getting.

Good advice is advice you feel is given with your best interest in mind. You will be the best judge, therefore, of whether the advice is good advice.

IN CONCLUSION

*Circumstances are beyond human control, but
our conduct is in our own power.*

—Benjamin Disraeli, British statesman

Whatever your circumstances, whatever your nature or the habits you've developed over time, you can evolve. It is not going to be without its struggles. Holocaust survivor Viktor Emil Frankl, MD, PhD, wrote in his 1946 memoir, *Man's Search for Meaning*, "Everything can be taken from a man but one thing: the last of the human freedoms—to choose one's attitude in any given set of circumstances, to choose one's own way." You are learning a new viewpoint about money and money management, and as you accept the mental and emotional concepts, your behavior in turn will change.  As you make your decisions concerning saving and spending money using a self-determined framework, you will act accordingly. Not overnight, not without mistakes, not without stumbling, but as you practice your new attitude and expertise, your chosen money attitude will become stronger. Your new framework for managing and acting within the sphere of money will grow and become more natural to you. Financial success, resilience, and growth will be your life. Success as *you* have defined it—not as chance allows.

Printed in the USA
CPSIA information can be obtained
at www.ICGtesting.com
JSHW011417160824
R13664500003B/R136645PG68134JSX00037B/17

9 781599 326313